LIFE AND DEATH AT WINDOVER:

EXCAVATIONS OF A 7,000-YEAR-OLD POND CEMETERY

RACHEL K. WENTZ

Life and Death at Windover:
Excavations of a 7,000-Year-Old Pond Cemetery

ISBN 10: 1-886104-55-7
ISBN 13: 978-1-886104-55-6

The Florida Historical Society Press
435 Brevard Avenue
Cocoa, FL 32922
www.myfloridahistory.org/fhspress

P•R•E•S•S

To Glen Doran

A mentor, a friend, and a slave driver.
Many thanks from your favorite student.

There are several people I would like to thank who made this book possible. I want to thank Jim Swann for his time and information, and for being such a conscientious environmentalist. Without his support, both financially and logistically, the site's excavations could never have proceeded. I want to thank those who shared their personal stories with me: Lynn Hansel, Bill Tanner, Steve Vanderjagt, Madeleine Carr, Richard Brunck, and Tom Penders. Your stories made this book possible. I want to thank Dave Dickel, whose skill and patience brought the Windover skeletons to the surface. And I want to thank Glen Doran, not only for his tireless dedication to the site's excavation, but for being such a guiding force in my education. Finally, I want to thank Greg, who has listened to me prattle on about Windover for the last eight years. Your support has been immeasurable and I love you for it.

TABLE OF CONTENTS

LIST OF ILLUSTRATIONS

Publisher's Preface

Created in 1856, the Florida Historical Society (FHS) is the oldest existing cultural organization in the state. We are dedicated to preserving Florida's past through the collection and archival maintenance of historical documents and photographs, through the publication of scholarly research on Florida history, and by educating the public about Florida history through a variety of public history projects. The FHS operates the Florida Historical Society Press which publishes a diverse selection of books, maintains an extensive archive in the Library of Florida History, and manages the historic Rossetter House Museum. We publish scholarly research in the *Florida Historical Quarterly*, produce *Florida Frontiers: The Weekly Radio Magazine of the Florida Historical Society*, and host many public events. Each May we hold our Annual Meeting and Symposium in a different Florida town, presenting scholarly paper presentations and roundtable discussions, tours of historic sites, an awards luncheon, and a banquet dinner. We are also the proud hosts of the Florida Public Archaeology Network (FPAN) East Central Region at our statewide headquarters in historic Cocoa Village.

Our collaboration with FPAN is a natural extension of more than a century of the FHS supporting archaeology in Florida. For example, the Florida Historical Society was the first statewide organization dedicated to the preservation of Florida history and prehistory as stated in our 1905 constitution. We were the first statewide organization to collect Native American relics such as stone pipes, hatchets, spear and arrowheads, and pottery, and we were the first statewide organization to actively promote and publish archaeological research dating back to

i

the 1930s. Amateur archaeologist Clarence B. Moore, who was very active in Florida, became a member of the FHS in 1907 and contributed his own written works to our library. We were instrumental in the creation of the position of Florida State Archaeologist and in the establishment of the Florida Anthropological Society in the 1940s.

This book, *Life and Death at Windover: Excavations of a 7,000-Year-Old Pond Cemetery*, written by FPAN East Central Region Director Dr. Rachel Wentz, is the first popular history of the incredible Windover Archaeological Dig and the amazing discoveries it uncovered. While the book *Windover: Multidisciplinary Investigations of an Archaic Florida Cemetery* (University Press of Florida, 2002), edited by Dr. Glen H. Doran, is a fascinating collection of scientific papers by professional archaeologists and other specialists, it is not easily accessible to a general audience. This new book by Dr. Wentz tells the fascinating story of Windover from the initial discovery of human remains at the site through the conclusion of the excavation process and beyond. The story is told through the eyes of the participants, from construction workers and real estate developers to professional archaeologists. The author did the majority of her graduate work studying the Windover skeletons, and is now writing for a general audience from an insider's perspective.

The Windover site has been called "one of the most important archaeological discoveries in the world" because of the quantity and quality of the human remains and artifacts uncovered, which are 3,200 years older than King Tutankhamen and 2,000 years older than the Great Pyramid in Egypt. The presence of intact brain matter in more than ninety skulls, tools made of animal bone and other materials, and some of the oldest woven fabric found anywhere all add to the significance of this archaeological site. It is important to note that the Windover Dig would probably not happen today with the current federal laws regarding the excavation of Native American remains. It may be one of the last such archaeological excavations to take place in the United States.

The Florida Historical Society Press is publishing this book in conjunction with the thirtieth anniversary of the initial discovery of the

Windover site. It is an appropriate time to reflect upon the lives of these prehistoric indigenous people of Florida, who lived and died in the same area where, many centuries later, pioneer cattleman made homesteads, educator and civil rights activist Harry T. Moore worked for racial equality, and every manned mission into space originating from the United States was launched. The story of Windover is an essential portion of the history of people in Florida.

Dr. Ben Brotemarkle
Executive Director
Florida Historical Society
March 2012

A photograph of the Windover bog as seen today. Photo by Wentz.

SECTION ONE

GETTING STARTED

Dawn breaks over a small pond in eastern Florida as the early rays from a late summer sun pierce the dense scrub of pines and palmettos. It is seven thousand years ago. The construction of the Egyptian pyramids is two thousand years in the future. Writing has yet to be invented and agriculture has yet to emerge in most of the world. But near the eastern coast of Central Florida in the present-day city of Titusville, a small group of ancient Floridians are gathering at this secluded body of water for the burial of their dead.

The pond is rimmed by rugged flora native to the area. Pond willow, cattails, and dog fennel line its outskirts, while inland, cabbage palms and saw grass spread like an impenetrable blanket over the sandy soils. The area is shaded by the outstretched limbs of hickories and pines. The group huddles together in a solemn circle as a low mist glides along the mirrored surface of the pond and the smell of wood smoke permeates the air. They mourn quietly, each of them familiar with the grief of loss. This will be the final resting place for a young boy who will join the many who have gone before him. Like them, he will be wrapped in woven matting and placed beneath the surface of the pond. The dark waters will enclose his fragile remains for thousands of years.

Fast-forward seven thousand years to a warm day in late spring 1982. The early summer winds are stripping the fading azalea blooms from their branches, spreading them in colorful blankets across the ground, as a man walks into a restaurant carrying a human skull. He is not a criminal, not a scientist, but a backhoe operator tasked with clearing the soft peats from the base of a nearby pond. As he was depositing the dark spoils in a heap along the pond's western rim, the skull appeared, glinting in the morning sun.

The pond was one of many dotting the vast tract of land being cleared to make way for the new Windover Farms housing development. This pond would yield the remnants of early Floridians who lived and died

3

along its banks thousands of years ago. The skull would set in motion events leading to the discovery of one of the most significant archaeological sites in the world: Windover Pond.

My involvement with Windover would come twenty years later. When the site was discovered, I was just finishing high school and had no plans of becoming an archaeologist. In fact, I had never even heard of archaeology's parent discipline, anthropology, until I stumbled across it in the University of Central Florida's course catalog.

I enrolled at UCF and began coursework toward a BA in anthropology. But having already spent two years in college drifting through an associate's degree, I was anxious to begin a career. So I switched gears, deciding instead to become a firefighter/paramedic and going to work for the Orlando Fire Department.

But after a decade of blood, guts, and fire, I was ready for something a bit more cerebral, a job that didn't involve rushing into burning buildings or tending the angry transients that populated Orlando's west side. Having completed my BA, I applied to the graduate program in anthropology at Florida State University, was accepted, retired from the fire department, packed up my belongings, and headed north. It was as a new graduate student at FSU that I first met the people from Windover.

Anthropology, "the study of man," is composed of four sub-disciplines. Cultural anthropology examines the origins, dissemination, and idiosyncrasies of human culture; linguistics is the study of human language; archaeology is the study of humans based on their material remains recovered through excavation; and biological anthropology, traditionally known as physical anthropology, examines humans from a biological perspective.

Bioarchaeology is a sub-discipline of biological anthropology and examines issues of health through the analysis of human remains recovered from archaeological sites. I wanted to be a bioarchaeologist.

The human skeleton is a guide to the life history of the individual, every surface a landscape of biological clues. My background in medicine instinctively drew me to the field of bioarchaeology, in which I

4

learned the science and art of human skeletal analysis. It was during my early training as a bioarchaeologist that I came to know the people from Windover. Their skeletons were housed within the Department of Anthropology at FSU, carefully stored within sturdy metal cabinets in a secured lab. Through endless hours of analysis over the next few years, I would come to know each of them. Their bones would be my guide to the past.

The excellent preservation at Windover was the result of chemistry and luck. The dark peats within the base of the pond that held the remains provided the perfect environment for the preservation of skeletal tissue: a neutral pH and very little oxygen. It is this remarkable preservation that has enabled a glimpse into the health and history of each individual, since many of their bones are intact, many of the skeletons complete.

My years as a medic instilled in me a fascination with traumatic injury. I considered trauma patients the most complex to treat and stabilize. Shattered bone from gunshot wounds, crushing injuries from car crashes—the field of emergency medicine provided an endless variety of force-related wounds. I applied my fascination to the Windover skeletons. My master's thesis examined their fractures: how many of the individuals had sustained broken bones during life and which of their bones were most commonly broken. I was also curious about what had caused these injuries; whether the fractures were the result of accidents, such as falls, or the result of violence, since blunt-force trauma can be indicative of combat.

The trauma analysis was just the beginning. With each bit of information I gathered, new questions arose. I wanted to know more about their overall health. My dissertation examined a full spectrum of pathologies, from dental disease to arthritis, infection to nutritional stress. Every aspect of my research involved spending hours poring over each of the ten thousand bones that make up this remarkable population.

I came to know them personally. I knew them by age: the fragile bones of the newborns that never made it to their first birthday; the elderly who somehow managed to live into their fifties, their joints frozen by arthritis, their teeth worn and falling out. I knew them by their sex: the robust, muscular frames of the males; the gracile yet sturdy bones of the females; both sexes exhibiting the tell-tale signs of a physically demanding life. But most of all I came to know them by their pathologies: the woman with the broken femur who managed to heal from this serious injury, yet lived with a significant limp that would have made gathering food a difficult and painful endeavor; the young boy with spina bifida whose emaciated legs would never have allowed him to walk or run.

Each of the individuals represented someone who lived thousands of years in the past, yet suffered from the same illnesses and injuries we encounter today. They did it without modern medicine, without surgical intervention. They lived in a time that predated some of our most fundamental cultural inventions: pottery, metallurgy, agriculture. These things were unknown to ancient people of Windover.

When I applied to Florida State, I had never heard of the Windover site. I didn't know that my advisor, Dr. Glen Doran, had led the excavations. It was good fortune; fate, if you believe in such things, but coming to FSU and being able to cut my teeth as a bioarchaeologist on such remarkable skeletons has been a unique opportunity, one that has shaped my future, guided my research.

I knew the basics of the site's discovery. The skeletons had surfaced during construction of a housing development in Titusville, Florida, back in the early 1980s. The excavations were conducted over three field seasons spanning 1984-86. I knew the pond's chemistry had allowed for exceptional preservation and that the well-preserved skeletons were accompanied by an array of grave goods. What I didn't know was the site's full story.

Only one book had been written about Windover. In 2000, Doran edited a massive technical volume, a compilation of research highlighting the multidisciplinary nature of the site's analysis. But for the average reader, the book is a behemoth full of statistics, tables, and technical jargon. I initially thought I could reduce the contents of Doran's book into something more palatable to the general public. But when my outline was complete, it seemed dry and academic. I had designated the chapters based on aspects of recovery within the excavations: site discovery, the skeletons, the material culture, the DNA analysis . . . (I'm dozing off just recounting it). This wouldn't work.

I needed a fresh approach, one that would take the reader through the incredible adventure of the site's discovery and the three field seasons of excavations that followed. So I deleted the old outline and decided that the only way I was going to recreate the events at Windover was to talk to those who were there. I wanted to step back in time and experience what the discovery and excavation of the site had been like for those involved. I wanted to meet the individuals whose labor had resulted in one of the most important archaeological sites in North America, if not the world. I wanted to return to Windover.

I had worked with Doran for many years, but we never really discussed the events surrounding the site. It seemed we were always too busy working on the skeletons to discuss their discovery and emergence from the pond. Doran had mentioned the people involved in the early stages of the site's discovery: Jim Swann, the powerful and influential land owner who donated much of the materials and machinery that facilitated excavations; Steve Vanderjagt, the backhoe operator who first noticed the pale bones within the spoils; Lynn Hansel and Bill Tanner, who worked for Swann, handling his land permits and overseeing construction crews within the development; and the many volunteers who were integral to the site's excavation. Their names were part of the history and lore of the site, ghost-like and ephemeral.

Besides Doran, I knew only one other person involved in the excavations. A bioarchaeologist with Florida's Bureau of Archaeological Research in Tallahassee, Dave Dickel had served as co-director of the project, overseeing the excavations and performing the initial analyses of the skeletons. As a graduate student, I consulted with Dave on skeletal projects since he had a sharp eye and a wealth of experience when it came to pathological analysis of human remains. He was also a colorful character with a curious perspective on science and life. But we never really discussed Windover.

I wanted to know what it was like at the moment of discovery. What did it feel like to be the first to set eyes on a skull that had been tucked away in a pond for thousands of years? How did it feel to cut through those dense layers of peat, revealing the beautifully preserved body of an ancient Floridian and be the first to touch the bones of someone who lived so long ago? What were those long days like under sun-scorched skies as the field crews toiled within the soft base of the pond? And what was it like at the end of the final field season, to stand and watch the water, held at bay by an extensive network of pumps, return to the pond, slowly covering the soils that had protected the people of Windover for so long?

I needed to track down the individuals I didn't know and sit down and talk with those I did. With their help, I could recreate the early events at Windover, the day the first skull appeared in the spoils, and how the events of the next few years would lead to one of the most incredible archaeological finds in the world. This would be their story: the story of Windover pond.

CAST OF CHARACTERS

I met Jim Swann on a hot day in early July. I pulled up in front of his office—a low, square building painted crystalline blue—pressed the buzzer and waited to be admitted. I was let in by one of his assistants, a soft-spoken woman who guided me into the lobby. I stood and waited for Jim to descend the stairway that led from his offices on the second floor. The lobby opened to offices in the back, a conference room to the left, the stairway to the right. The walls of the lobby sported newspaper articles about Swann, touting his extensive commitments to environmentalism within Brevard County, an unusual trait for a land developer. I was a bit nervous. I had met Swann once, years ago at an event celebrating the Windover site. He was a man of few words; a "no B.S." type of individual.

Swann is an influential figure in the area, an active member in numerous environmental and philanthropic organizations. He has served as chairman of The Nature Conservancy, president of the Brevard Zoo, and chairman of the Marine Resources Council, just to name a few. He has also served as board member for a number of organizations within the county. His development company, EKS, Inc., was founded in 1979. He is a busy man.

He came down the stairs, a lean individual with snowy white beard and hair, eyes of icy blue. I knew he must be at least in his sixties by now, since the Windover project was almost thirty years in the past, but he moved like a younger man and had a look in his eyes that said, "Don't waste my time."

We sat down at the oval glass-topped table in the conference room. I took out my tape recorder, which he eyed with suspicion, and explained that I had a short list of questions that would help me illuminate the events surrounding the site's discovery. He replied, "I really don't remember anything." With a nervous gulp, I turned on the recorder as he proceeded to talk for the next forty-five minutes.

Swann was born in Tampa, Florida, where he grew up along the shores of Tampa Bay. An outdoorsman at an early age, he was destined to be a developer. His grandfather had emigrated from Tennessee to work as a developer in Tampa where he built the four-and-a-half-mile Bayshore Boulevard, the world's longest continual sidewalk; Hyde Park, which today is the center of Tampa's nightlife, with its rows of restaurants and bars; and Florida's largest cargo tonnage port, Port Tampa. Development was "in the family blood."

When he was seven, his father died suddenly of a heart attack. Two years later, his mother remarried "an up-and-coming businessman named Jack Eckerd," whose father, J. Milton Eckerd, founded the famed Eckerd chain of drugstores in 1898. Jack moved the family to Clearwater, where Swann spent the rest of his childhood.

Swann honed his skills in development at an early age. In college, he purchased old buildings, restored them, and turned them into student apartments. In 1970, he fell in love with Brevard County, which he considered more "active and vibrant" than many of the other seaside counties in Florida. His home of Pinellas County was quickly becoming a retirement haven; Brevard hosted a younger population, one in which he could establish his business and "get away from all the people."

In the late 1970s, a realtor friend told him about a large tract of land in north Brevard whose owners were anxious to sell. The property, located in the southern end of the small town of Titusville, straddled a vast strip of land between the St. Johns River to the west and US 1 to the east. The property would be the ideal spot for a large community serving the residents of Titusville, who were coming in droves to work at nearby Kennedy Space Center (KSC).

Swann put in a low bid offer of $380 per acre. The owners accepted the bid on Thursday, subject to closing the following Monday. The tract totaled sixty-five hundred acres, about a third of which would be slated for the new Windover Farms housing development. Following the purchase, one could walk from US 1, all the way to the St Johns River and, with the exception of I-95 and Highway 407, would not have stepped foot off of EKS land.

The sellers, a family called Tisch, were liquidating their assets in order to purchase a large insurance company. The insurance company fell through, so they took their millions and bought CBS instead, greatly expanding their family's fortune. Swann tells people, "I made the Tisch family rich."

Windover Farms began with a road. Windover Way would wind through over fifteen hundred acres of dense pine and oak forests, over five hundred of which would be set aside for conservation. The main road would eventually branch off into smaller roads that would serve over six hundred spacious lots.

Back then, south Titusville was practically uninhabited. Founded in 1867, Titusville was named after Confederate Colonel Henry Theodore Titus, who won the right to name the town by defeating his opponents in a game of dominoes. A century later, the city strived to keep pace with the growing space industry. Its population increased by over three hundred percent between 1960 and 1970 as the space industry boomed. The decade opened with the launch of the newly developed Delta rocket. A year later, Alan Shepard made his monumental flight to become the first American in space. That same year, President Kennedy gave his historic speech in which he announced plans to go to the moon. The decade culminated with Neil Armstrong being the first to step foot on its surface in July 1969. It was an electric period in America's race to space.

Swann needed a way to lure people to south Titusville. His plan: The Roost, a small two-story building he constructed at the entrance to Windover Farms. The upper floor would house his offices; the lower level would serve as a lunch counter. Each morning, the two women who ran the counter would flour, knead, and bake the scrumptious rolls on which they would serve a variety of sandwiches. The smell of fresh-baked bread would waft from their small kitchen, spreading through the nearby forest, as hungry workers from KSC made their way across the causeway for lunch each day. Lunchtime was a family affair; everyone in the office pitched in to serve customers, including Swann and his secretary. The restaurant's slogan was "If you like my sandwiches, you'll love my lots!" It would be at The Roost, on that warm day in 1982, that Swann would first set eyes on the ancient remains from Windover.

From a distance, Lynn Hansel could be mistaken for Jim Swann. Like Swann, he sports a white beard and locks, and has a lean, energetic frame. His eyes are also a deep blue, yet they lack the icy intensity of Jim's. Lynn's are the calming blue of the Caribbean; they flash when he spins his tales.

I met Lynn at his home, a ten-acre spread that was part of EKS's original tract. His house, a comfortable, single-story ranch, looks out over scrub forest from which white-tailed deer emerge each evening. As we made our introductions, standing in the shade on the long drive that loops in front of his house, wild turkeys scratched at the earth under distant oaks and red-tailed hawks called overhead.

He invited me into his small office, adjacent to a garage stuffed with the toys of an outdoorsman: four-wheelers, a boat, fishing gear, a golf cart; everything one would need for playing in the woods. The office was a narrow rectangle with tables built down one side. A large air conditioner hummed in the back of the room, a welcome relief from the intense noonday heat. We sat down, I turned on the tape recorder, and he began his story.

Lynn is an Iowa native. Although raised an Air Force brat, in the late sixties he returned to Iowa where he completed a bachelor's degree in urban and regional planning at Iowa State. He wound up in Brevard County to be close to his parents; they were stationed at Patrick Air Force Base where his father served as the base's civil engineer. He interned with Brevard County Planning Division and eventually went to work for them full time. He was later employed as Planning Director for the City of Titusville. He was feeling burned out in his profession when a friend of his suggested, "You should meet a guy named Jim Swann. You two might get along." He met Swann, they got along, and Lynn went to work for him in 1978.

Like Swann, Lynn loves the outdoors. He enjoys tromping through the woods, "looking at tracks and bones and fur and feathers." He and Jim are avid enthusiasts of the red-cockaded woodpecker.

While working for Swann, Lynn was responsible for initial site planning and coordinating environmental permitting for Swann's projects. He served as environmental liaison between EKS and numerous governmental agencies: the St. Johns Water Management District, the Army Corp of Engineers, local governments, and the state's Department of Environmental Protection. He attributes his success as a planner to his "easygoing gift of gab." He describes Swann as "a most conscientious" developer. Together, they have worked to save trees and open spaces, incorporating both into the planning and design of their projects.

Lynn did not have an office at The Roost. He was relegated to a battered trailer tucked in an oak hammock about a hundred yards from the restaurant. The office consisted of a narrow main room with plywood desks lining one wall, two bedrooms stuffed with boxes and gear, a non-functioning bathroom, and an extremely leaky roof. On cold mornings in the trailer, the first to arrive would build a fire in the wood stove purchased from Montgomery Ward. The stove's exhaust pipe ran the length of the ceiling, providing radiant heat throughout the rustic abode. With no running water, bathroom breaks involved slipping out back to the woods or, for emergency situations, a quick trip to The Roost. Lynn shared the office with the man responsible for day-to-day construction operations on site, Bill Tanner.

Bill Tanner is the type of person you immediately like upon meeting. I visited him at his home in Christmas, Florida, where he and his wife, Diane, live on a large plot of land he inherited from his father. The original spread encompassed about four thousand acres, which his father purchased back in the 1930s for fifty cents an acre. At the entrance to his drive stands the family home, now vacant and in the process of being consumed by the nearby forest. He speaks with a pronounced twang passed down by his ancestors from Coffee County, Georgia. His great-great grandfather was the first circuit judge in the area, back when eastern Orange County was part of the dubiously named Mosquito County, which stretched all the way to the coast. Christmas is a tight-knit community. For decades, Fort Christmas

13

Park, located just up the road, served as the meeting place for a four-day Fourth of July festival that drew thousands of visitors. Riders on horseback would come from as far north as Jacksonville, as far south as Okeechobee, for the annual gathering.

Bill is built for the construction industry, with the sturdy frame of a draft horse. Powerful arms and legs sprout from his thick torso and he pads around his property on bare feet. He is warm and welcoming, the type of individual I immediately wanted to sit down with over a beer. We head inside his immaculate home, where Diane flits around the room in constant motion. She is his polar opposite in build; a willowy woman with a youthful figure. Bill and I take our places at the dining room table and begin.

Bill met Swann while clearing one of the new lots within the Windover Farms subdivision. He had been hired by the lot's owner and was busy manipulating his front-end loader when he noticed a man with white hair and a steely gaze, standing off to the side, watching him work. Feeling a bit disconcerted, he continued clearing. When the man showed up the next day, Bill got a bit nervous.

"May I help you?"

The man replied, "No."

Bill continued to work until his curiosity got the better of him. He drove the loader down to where the man was standing.

"Is there anything I can do for you?" Bill inquired.

"I'm just watching you work."

"Am I doin' all right?" he said, gazing down from his machine.

"Yes, but you're slow," the stranger replied.

"That may be true," Bill said, "but I don't kill trees."

When those magic words fell on Swann's ears, he knew Bill was the right man for the job.

Bill had been running heavy machinery since about the age of ten. If it had a steering wheel and gears, he could drive it. He initially worked for Swann clearing right-of-ways and installing municipal water lines. Over time, he oversaw construction activities throughout the development. With Lynn orchestrating planning and permitting, and Bill handling the day-to-day operations, both under the watchful eye of Swann,

Windover Farms slowly emerged from the scrub. But as the road progressed, they frequently encountered mucky areas needing to be filled. What they needed was a skilled backhoe operator. Then they found Steve Vanderjagt.

It took me about three weeks to track down Steve. As he was the first individual to set eyes on the skeletons at Windover, his account was critical to my story. I tried several phone numbers I found on the internet, all of which had been disconnected. By the time I met with Bill Tanner, I had almost given up hope of finding him. But as Bill and I settled in for his interview, the first thing he said was "I found Steve!"

Bill had tracked him down through various acquaintances in the construction biz, finally obtaining a number for Steve's home in Grant-Valkaria, a small community just south of Melbourne, Florida. I called, left a message, and waited. It didn't take long. Steve called me back that evening and we set up a time to meet. The following week, I travelled south along US 1, through barren expanses of burnt snags left over from wildfires that had blown through the area four years ago, until I finally pulled onto his expansive property.

Steve and his wife, Donna, live on what some would call a compound. Their house is set off the road, tucked among numerous small outbuildings that house machinery along with a lifetime of paperwork: employment records, business receipts, old time cards; ammunition against a potential IRS audit. Donna seldom throws anything away.

The Vanderjagt home is a disjointed collection of history. The walls are lined with high, narrow shelves stuffed with knick-knacks and collectibles; mostly antique tins, handmade boxes, and children's toys from a bygone era. One could spend a full day wandering through their home and still not see everything; a history buff's delight.

Steve bares the tell-tale signs of someone who has spent a lifetime working outdoors. His skin is permanently stained a dark tan. His sandy hair is close cropped in military fashion and he sports faded tattoos on his left arm and chest. Straddling the bridge of his nose is an impressive scar, the result of too many years in the sun and the sharp blade of a dermatologist. His wife, Donna, is warm and talkative, with

15

sporty, pale blond hair. They would make the perfect pioneer couple, sturdy and self-reliant. They met over fifty years ago, at a drive-in burger stand when Donna was still in high school. They've been together ever since. Like many couples long married, they finish each other's sentences.

The three of us sat down at their kitchen table for the interview. A small passel of cats bustled about the kitchen, crying to be let out and then crying to get back in. On the table sat a worn photo album; before I could even ask, Donna flipped it open, producing faded photos of the first skeletons to come out of the ground at Windover.

They had many photos of the site in its early stages, when it was just a small, mucky pond, before it was peeled open by archaeologists. I was finally going to get a first-hand account of the discovery of the skeletons I'd spent the last ten years working on.

Steve's story began two generations ago when his grandfather, a seventeen-year-old stowaway, hitched a ride on a freighter bound for America. He left behind his home in Holland to pursue a life in the States, and eventually accumulated enough capital to start a farm. There, he raised horses and Christmas trees. Each winter, he would cut down his trees, load them on a flatbed, and haul them to Detroit, where they were sold at auction.

Steve was born in Cadillac, Michigan, but spent his adult years in Detroit. His was a mobile childhood. His father, a foreman for a large contracting company, followed the work. The family lived in a trailer that moved throughout Michigan as his father oversaw construction projects on the state's highways. Wherever there were new roads to be built, the Vanderjagts were not far behind.

Steve was introduced to heavy equipment at an early age. He started working construction at the age of sixteen on his father's projects, first learning how to drive a front-end loader, later graduating to a backhoe. He eventually purchased his own equipment and went into business for himself.

Steve and Donna came to Florida in 1981 to escape the bad economy further north. They brought with them two kids, a cat named Kitty, and a backhoe. He was hired by Clark & Sons Construction for five dollars an hour. The job he had left in Detroit had paid twenty-five an hour. He told Donna the move had been a terrible mistake. He took the job anyway, running a backhoe the company rented from a local agency. Since he owned his own backhoe, Steve persuaded Clark & Sons that the cost of renting the machine could be put to better use in his pocket. They agreed and from that point on he used his own equipment.

While still working for the construction company, he was approached by Nelson Real Estate about a job up in Titusville. The firm needed someone to clear several lots they had recently purchased within the new Windover Farms development. Steve accepted the job and toted his backhoe north. It was on a fortuitous day in early 1982, while clearing lots for Nelson, that he was approached by Bill Tanner, who just happened to be looking for a backhoe operator, as well.

Steve took the job with Bill, working in concert with crews clearing trees and brush, using his backhoe to fill in low areas that stood in the path of Windover Way. They had gone through several mucky areas when they came upon a small pond that would turn out to be a bit more complicated than the others. They had no idea what was waiting for them in the muck.

A SKULL IN THE SPOILS

The day began like many others. Steve approached the pond, noting the telltale indicators of wet ground: saw grass and flat sedge extending from moist, dark soils. The pond, which stretched about two hundred feet across, was actually a small alcove formed from seeping groundwater and overflow from nearby Bird Lake Marsh. As a bulldozer and loader worked on the nearby roadbed, Steve positioned his backhoe at the rim of the pond.

He began by constructing his "bridge"—an area he built up using nearby brush so that the backhoe could work without sinking into the soft muck. He then began digging into the inky-black soils. As he worked, he watched. Years of experience had taught him that strange things sometimes emerged from holes in the ground. In the past, his

Vanderjagt uses his backhoe to clear the area for Windover Way. Photo courtesy of G. Doran.

digging had produced "bowling balls"—large, smooth stones transported miles from their source by the action of glaciers; rusted pieces of antique machinery; even a large whale bone, which ended up on display on the Vanderjagt lawn.

As he made a "pass" with his bucket, scooping the soft peats from the base of the pond, carefully unfolding the soils onto the spoil bank, a pale rock the size of a cantaloupe rolled from the bucket, down the side of the mound. Curious, Steve climbed down from the machine, making his way along the spoils to where the rock had settled. He reached down and picked it up. As he turned it over in his hands, two black sockets stared back at him. His first thought: "Oh, shit!"

He knew the head must have a body, so he climbed back onto the backhoe and made another pass. As the muck exited his bucket, so did another skull and several longbones. He knew it was time to call for backup.

The bones set off a chain reaction. Steve told Bill, Bill told Lynn, Lynn called Swann, and roadwork screeched to a halt. Steve, carrying the skeletons in a bucket, headed for The Roost, where he presented the remains to Swann.

Hoping for guidance from law enforcement, Swann carried the bones across the street to the Highway Patrol station. According to Swann, they were met with a chilly reception. The troopers took one look at the skeletons and said, "We only do car wrecks."

They returned to The Roost, where they contemplated their next move. In the meantime, a storm was brewing. The skies turned black, the wind picked up, and the crew grew nervous as the area around the pond darkened. One of the younger crew members, Lester Canada, had just started working for Bill. Bill had known the Canada family for many years as they were also residents of Christmas. Lester was a gifted musician. On rainy days, the crew would huddle inside the leaky trailer as Lester entertained them with whatever instrument he happened to have in his truck that day. If the instrument had strings, Lester could play it.

The Canada family was a highly superstitious bunch. Knowing that, Bill should have anticipated the reaction of young Lester following the discovery of the skeletons. But the day had been one of mystery and turmoil. The last thing on Bill's mind was the emotional state of his young crew member.

As Bill and the crew headed from the pond to The Roost, hoping to get out of the weather, lightening flashed and loose palm fronds scudded across Windover Way. The woods that lined the road grew dark. Shadows lurked and lightening illuminated the darker recesses in strobe-like pulses. As their truck came around a bend, they saw Lester heading in their direction at a full run. The rain had begun to fall and the crew assumed Lester was running for shelter. But as they approached him, they noted the fear in his eyes, the look of terror on his face. They stopped the truck, narrowly avoiding hitting him as he reigned in his pace as he reached the side of the truck.

"I just saw three Indians running across the road!" he stammered. "They's 'haints' in these woods!"

The wind-blown palm fronds and shadowy movement from the forest had worked him into such a panic, he was seeing ghosts at every turn. He couldn't get into the truck fast enough. Later, when Bill instructed him to return to the pond, Lester vowed he would quit before he would set foot near the site of the skeletons.

Not only did the storm scare the hell out of Lester, it also revealed more bones. When the rain stopped falling, the crew (minus Lester) headed back to the pond. Among the spoils, numerous bones protruded from the soft peat, rinsed clean from the rain. The crew gathered what they could, placing the remains in five-gallon buckets of water to keep the bones moist. Now what?

Swann called the county coroner. A sheriff's detective and the assistant Coroner came out to have a look around. They tentatively poked around the pond, collected the bones, and left. A couple of days later, curious about the disposition of the bones, Lynn called the coroner's office. He was told the bones were not those of modern-day Floridians; that they were simply "old bones." Lynn passed the information on to Swann, who then wanted to know when they would get the bones back. Lynn dialed the coroner's office again, requesting the bones be returned. The coroner was perplexed; no one ever wanted bones back.

Two of the first skulls discovered in the pond. Photo courtesy of G. Doran.

Lynn argued with the coroner, demanding their return. After a phone call from one of Swann's business associates, who just happened to be chief medical examiner for the state of Florida, the bones were returned and placed back in their five-gallon holding cells, where they remained for the next few months.

The buckets initially resided in Swann's garage. After a short period, their presence began to give Jim the creeps, so he relocated the buckets to the dilapidated trailer. They sat just inside the front door of the trailer, close enough to the entrance that crews were constantly stubbing their toes on the heavy containers. Lynn and Bill took turns refilling the buckets, checking on the bones as their water levels dropped.

Something had to be done. The bones couldn't stay in the trailer forever. Aside from that, Swann was genuinely curious about the pond and what might still be hidden in the muck. They needed guidance; they needed professionals; they needed an archaeologist.

They contacted the University of Florida. Dr. Brenda Sigler-Eisenberg, an archaeologist, and Dr. William Maples, one of the state's most renowned forensic anthropologists, visited the site. Upon his arrival at

UF in 1972, Maples began making a name for himself as a forensic anthropologist, eventually founding the CA Pound Human Identification Lab, located on UF's campus. Perhaps Maples had bigger things on his mind when he visited the Windover site, for he and Sigler-Eisenberg took one look at the bones and one look at the pond before deciding to pass.

Keep in mind what they saw at the time of their visit. Although numerous well-preserved bones had been recovered from the spoils, Maples and Sigler-Eisenberg had no idea how old the bones were. In addition, the site itself was problematic. Since the bones had come from within the pond, excavations would have to be carried out in order to determine how many more skeletons were still tucked within the muck. The most difficult thing about doing archaeology in a pond is, of course, the water. What do you do with all that water? You would have to drain the pond in order to excavate, which would be time consuming and expensive, even if you could figure out a practical way of getting it done. And what if you went to all that trouble and expense, only to discover that the few skeletons pulled from the spoils were all that the pond held?

Even if you found more skeletons within the pond, they were more than likely a jumbled mess. The skeletons would probably have become "commingled" over time, mixing as the base of the pond shifted and settled. Without discrete graves, much of the archaeological information would be lost, for graves are treasure troves of information.

Graves speak of rituals performed within a society. The body's orientation (which direction the grave faces), its position (whether it is laid out or tucked into a bundle, face up or face down), and associated grave goods (what items are buried with the individual) provide clues as to who the person was, what they might have done in life, and what role they may have played within their society. Known as "mortuary analysis," the examination of graves provides the majority of archaeological information about ancient civilizations and is fundamental to interpreting past lives.

Grave goods can indicate gender and status. Weapons, tools, ceramics, and objects of adornment buried with an individual reflect the individual's role they played in society. Caches of elaborate grave goods may indicate elevated rank; objects associated with ritual, such as medicine bundles or sacred items, might indicate a spiritual leader within the group. Just as today, our burials say much about the dead and the society in which they lived.

But could this information be maintained within the base of a pond, whose water levels had most likely fluctuated over time, where the individuals in the pond would have shifted and mingled, and where it was unknown how many graves were originally interred? Sigler-Eisenberg was more interested in the adjacent hammock. On the southeast edge of the pond, a small oak hammock overlaid a natural rise in the landscape. About eighteen feet high at its point, the hammock might hold remnants of living sites associated with the people from Windover. She was all for testing the hammock, but as for the pond, it was just too problematic.

At this point we must take a moment to appreciate the unusual extent to which Swann went in order to find out more about the pond's inhabitants. Had this been any other developer, the bones would probably have been discretely covered up and work would have continued. Finding skeletons in the midst of a construction project is a developer's worst nightmare. It means work comes to a stop, authorities must be called in, and in some cases the project can be delayed indefinitely. Swann could have let it go once Maples visited the site. The bones could have merely been covered up, the road diverted, and the project continued. But Swann was genuinely curious about the people of Windover. How ancient were the remains? How many people were buried in the pond? And why did they choose such an unusual form of burial?

Swann had questions and he wanted answers. What he needed was to find someone undaunted by the site's complexity; someone as curious as he was about these most unusual burials; an individual who was just getting started in his career, someone young and hungry. So he contacted Florida State University and he found Glen Doran.

The note was scribbled on a piece of paper: some bones had been found in Brevard County and would he please follow up with a phone call. Doran glanced at the piece of paper, noted it had come directly from FSU's President's office, and called the number. He spoke with Lynn Hansel, who explained their situation and asked if Doran could come down and take a look. This wasn't the first time Doran had received calls about the discovery of human remains. He'd had similar experiences in his home state of Texas.

Midland is a small city jutting from the vast Southern Plains of west Texas. It was originally founded in 1881 as Midway Station because of its equidistance along the Texas and Pacific Railway line between the towns of Fort Worth and El Paso. The small, sleepy cattle town was dramatically transformed in 1923 when the Santa Rita No. 1 well began spewing oil from deep within the Permian Basin. Today, the basin produces a fifth of our nation's petroleum.

Doran was born and raised in Midland, where his parents ran a produce house selling chickens and eggs. Perhaps it was a lifetime surrounded by fowl that steered Doran in the direction of animal science. He attended the University of Texas at Austin, majoring in zoology and working in a lab. He boasts, "I can still dissect a salamander into thirty-five parts if you give me a good scalpel and scissors."

Along with his science courses, he took electives in anthropology. Over time, he realized his electives were far more interesting than his major, so he made the switch to anthropology, combining his love of biology and his interest in archaeology by specializing in bioarchaeology. It was as an undergrad that he heard about summer job opportunities with the Texas Highway Department. The Department was just starting its archaeology division and was looking for cheap summer help. Doran applied immediately.

He jumped at the chance to work in the field as an archaeologist. As roads were planned, he would perform archaeological surveys ahead of construction crews, looking for traces of ancient Texans. One such ancient Texan had originated from his small hometown.

Discovered in 1953 by pipeline worker and amateur archaeologist, Keith Glasscock, the remains were immediately labeled "Midland Man." The ancient skull was found in close association with extinct ice-age animals and ancient stone points. Later found to be a female, the skull was dated at around eleven thousand years and has been described as having a long, narrow head and very bad teeth.

Doran spent his summers with the Highway Department, traveling throughout the state on road projects. When he entered UT's graduate program, he worked for the Department full-time. On occasion, they would receive calls from field crews who had stumbled upon human remains. One such call turned out to be an abandoned slave cemetery, discovered during gravel mining. When the calls came, Doran would head to the site, determine where the remains were coming from, and try to figure out how old they were so the project could get back underway. "You hang around archaeology circles long enough, everyone gets those kinds of calls." So he assumed the skeletons from Titusville would be business as usual.

But summer was underway and Doran was getting ready for a National Park Service project in Pensacola: a prehistoric site within Gulf Island National Seashore near Escambia Bay. Bogged down in the details of field logistics, he promised Lynn he would make it down to Titusville as soon as he could break away. Once the Gulf Island project was completed, Doran headed east to Titusville. With him were Bruce Piatek, a graduate student and field assistant, and Robert Dailey, a fellow faculty member at FSU. They drove down together to check out the site.

Upon their arrival at Windover, they met up with Lynn and Bill and followed them down the narrow, dirt road that wound through the woods to the pond. As they approached the pond, Doran noticed that the road was bordered by a "long line of stinking black peat, rotting and decomposing in the sun." The spoil stretched about one hundred and fifty feet and stood about five feet tall. They got out and walked along the spoil, noting the jumbled layers of stratified earth, distinct in their various colors. Every fifteen to twenty feet, a small cluster of skeletal material would appear, pale against the dark earth. Doran thought, "Now THIS is getting interesting!"

They collected material from two areas around the pond: the smaller spoil to the eastern margin of the pond, and the larger spoil on the western side, in which the majority of the material was recovered.

Many of the remains were fragmented. They recovered a clavicle, two ulnas, a tibia, a radius, three fibulas, a piece of a jaw, a few ribs, and several unidentifiable pieces of bone. They also recovered a tool made of antler, a hint at the wealth of grave goods that would eventually be found buried alongside many of the individuals in the pond.

Doran could tell the remains were prehistoric from the heavy wear on the teeth, a trait typical of ancient populations whose diets consisted of gritty foods and who habitually used their teeth as tools. Once they had plucked the pale bones from the muck, they gathered the buckets of bones Bill and Lynn had brought from their trailer and packaged all of it for transport to FSU. Doran then boarded a bus for the long ride back to Tallahassee. While on the bus, Doran pulled a yellow legal pad from his bag and began making notes, mulling over what they had just seen.

Doran was on board. Swann encouraged him to write up a research proposal to try to obtain funding from FSU to conduct excavations. In the meantime, Windover Way was shifted westward in order to avoid more skeletons. But with the first dip of Steve's backhoe, more skeletons appeared. The road was shifted once again and work was able to proceed.

Doran told Swann he could prepare a more compelling proposal if they knew how old the bones were. Radiocarbon dating of the remains would provide a firm date. The problem was that Doran lacked the money to pay for it. Swann graciously volunteered to pay the several hundred dollars for a sample of bone to be dated. The sample, a few rib fragments, was sent to Beta Analytic, a radiocarbon dating firm in Coral Gables, Florida. When the date came back, Doran was sure there must have been a mistake, for the reported age of the bone predated the Egyptian pyramids by over two thousand years. According to Beta Analytic, the bone was over seven thousand years old.

Everyone was stunned. Like a good scientist, Doran remained cautious. Perhaps the sample was contaminated by the ancient peat in which it was found. He wanted to be certain he was dealing with a truly ancient skeletal population. Doran asked Swann if they could send two more samples for dating. The bones went out, the dates came back;

seven thousand years stood firm. Doran could barely contain his excitement. Based on the dates, Windover just might be one of the most ancient cemeteries in the New World.

Doran calculated what they had thus far: well-preserved skeletons, dating to over seven thousand years old, apparently buried in the base of a small pond. Taken individually, any one of these factors would have been cause for excitement; taken as a whole, the site could be phenomenal.

Doran wrote up a thirty-five-page proposal, touting the pond's antiquity, its potential significance, and the impact such a site could have on studies of Florida's ancient past. His request for $167,000 for excavations and analysis was sent to the Dean of Arts and Sciences at FSU. But the proposal was denied due to "lack of internal funding for this type of research." Swann moved in. He contacted his friend, the powerful lobbyist, Guy Spearman, who approached representatives Clark Maxwell and W.E. Gardner, requesting the proposal be sent before the Florida legislature. During the 1983 session, the Senate and House passed the bill appropriating funds for the project. However, during the last hour of the last day of session, Governor Graham vetoed the bill. Swann was not to be deterred. He knew politics; if at first you don't succeed . . .

The proposal was revised during the summer and the new report, along with an increased budget of $240,000, was sent to Spearman, who passed it along to Representative Gardner to be reintroduced in the next session. Finally, the bill was passed and the project approved, yet with a reduced budget of $200,000, which was appropriated to Florida's Board of Regents for FSU to conduct initial archaeological investigations of the site. The Florida legislature would later provide funding for the next two years: $240,000 each for the 1985 and 1986 field seasons. The seasons would last from around August through January. With funding in place, the FSU Media Center kicked into high gear, preparing a news release that fueled local and national interest, even before the first shovel hit the ground.

With excavations slated to begin, Doran knew he couldn't handle the project on his own. He needed a co-director, a seasoned archaeologist who not only knew how to manage a site but someone who knew skeletons. He picked up the phone and called his old college buddy, Dave Dickel.

Dickel and Doran are alike in some ways, different in others. Their physical dissimilarities stand in stark contrast to their shared love of archaeology and their fascination with human skeletons. Doran is a burly individual who stands well over six feet, with a deep baritone softened around the edges by a Texas drawl. Dickel, on the other hand, is lean and scruffy and looks like he just stumbled off the bus from Woodstock.

Dickel started out as a cultural anthropologist, but migrated to biological anthropology, pursuing an interest in ancient disease and human adaptation. As a grad student, he heard about a Saturday field course in archaeology that his friend assured him "would be a gas." It was, and Dickel was hooked. Like Doran, he went on to split his time between working as a field archaeologist and pursuing skeletal projects when opportunities arose.

Dickel worked in California as "a dig bum." He lived out of a battered blue Volkswagen van, on which he spent many an evening in the field tinkering with the engine and replacing the patches of Bondo that covered the holes in its rusted frame. He went wherever the projects took him. He would spend months in the field working on a site, and then pack up for home to spend the next few months writing up his report. Although the work prolonged his PhD, he was eventually able to finish his degree while avoiding the trap of student loans.

Upon graduation, he started his own cultural resource management firm, Past Tense Archaeology. His unique combination of archaeological experience and skeletal knowledge meant his firm was perfectly suited for mitigating burial mounds. He could excavate a site, analyze the remains, and produce a comprehensive report, all on his own, without the need for outside specialists.

He and Doran met as PhD candidates on the bus that took them back and forth between the UC Davis campus and the Lowie Museum at Berkeley. An agricultural school, the university provided kitchen gardens for their students, many of whom came to rely on the gardens for survival. Glen and Dave were two such students; the gardens were central to their economy and they relied on the fruits and vegetables they produced to sustain them throughout the year.

The university also maintained poultry farms. Dickel would haul a trailer to the university's barns, shoveling manure from beneath hundreds of squawking chickens, and then tote it back to their gardens, where it was sprinkled among their burgeoning plots.

The fertile valleys of central California provided crops year-round and Dickel and Doran became serious farmers. What they didn't eat Dickel would take to nearby farmer's markets to be sold or used for barter. Yellow crookneck squash, red-leaf lettuce, an array of peppers (sweet and hot), white onions, and red potatoes sprang from their well-tended rows. The melons were the real money makers. Numerous types of watermelons—with seeds, without seeds, big, small, yellow, and green; musk melons and cantaloupes; any exotic species that caught Dickel's eye in the annual Burpee gardening catalog, which he "drooled over like it was a Playboy."

He and Doran became predatory when it came to the gardens. Always on the lookout for an abandoned plot, they would move in slowly at first. They would weed and water the neglected plot, and if no one showed up, they would eventually claim it as their own. Over time, they doubled their allotted space. Thus, dirt sustained them, as gardeners and as archaeologists.

When Doran called with news of the Windover skeletons, Dickel packed his (new) van and headed east. Knowing the "gutless wonder" VW would never make it cross-country, he decided the time was right for a new ride and traded in the old van for a sporty 1979 Ford Econoline. Although the new van broke down twice before crossing the California state line, it managed to transport him and his little dog Whippet (who ironically is a whippet) cross-country to Florida and the awaiting dig.

HOW TO DIG IN A POND

Two hundred thousand dollars may sound like a lot of money, but when you consider the cost of archaeological excavations, much less the additional costs of conducting excavations within a pond, funds disappear like water through a sieve. Fortunately for Doran, Swann was willing to shoulder some of the costs, as well as provide the heavy equipment necessary to work within the pond. First up was to secure the equipment and personnel.

Doran wrote out a detailed budget, listing in detail what would be needed. First on the list were personnel costs, which included his and Dickel's salaries and the salaries of research assistants and temporary workers that would accompany the archaeologists into the field. Then they would need monies for specialists, who would be paid as contractual workers. They included radiocarbon and amino acid dating of materials, faunal and floral analyses, geological sampling and processing, video and photography to record the excavations and burials, and a paleopathologic analysis of the remains once they were out of the ground. All of this wouldn't be cheap. Doran also had to add in the costs of travel, housing, utilities and phones, per diems for each worker, and finally field supplies. The money was dwindling quickly.

Once the equipment and personnel were in place, they addressed the issue of a laboratory. They would need a safe, secure site where the skeletons could be cleaned, stabilized, catalogued, and then stored. Fortunately, Brevard Community College's Cocoa campus, located about fifteen miles south of Titusville, volunteered lab space. The college would provide space throughout the three field seasons.

The next point of logistics to tackle was the pond itself. The skeletons at Windover had survived relatively intact for over seven thousand years because of one primary factor: the peat at the base of the pond. Peat is made up of layers of accumulated organics, primarily decomposing plant material, that form within low-lying, marshy areas. The acidic environments produced by peat, combined with low oxygen concentrations, slows decomposition of the organics. Over time, the layers of peat accumulate. More time means more layers, which in turn means more pressure as the weight of the material builds. With enough time (say, a few million years) and pressure (such as that found deep within the earth), peat is eventually transformed into coal.

At Windover, the peat provided a protective, anaerobic environment for the skeletons. But there was one other factor that contributed to their exceptional preservation: the pH. The pond in which the people from Windover chose to place their dead just happened to be of a neutral pH; an unusual occurrence in peat deposits, as Doran's team would later find when they tested the pH of nearby ponds, the majority of which were acidic. If the normal acidic conditions of peat had prevailed, the bones would have dissolved, as they do if placed in Florida's acidic soils. This combination of neutral pH and lack of oxygen formed the perfect environment for the preservation of skeletal material, allowing the bones at Windover to survive for thousands of years.

Even though the skeletons were well-preserved, the fact that they were dealing with a "wet site" held numerous complications. Wet sites present complex excavation scenarios; the archaeological materials themselves demand extra care. When materials are excavated from wet environments are exposed to air, they tend to degrade rapidly. That is why artifacts excavated from shipwrecks are transported in the water from which they came, so that the material's environment remains stable until they can be treated in the laboratory. Doran and Dickel knew the excavations at Windover would have to proceed slowly and cautiously. If the muck surrounding the burials was allowed to dry out, the bones would dry out as well, possibly cracking and warping. They also knew that whatever they removed from the pond would have to be protected during transport to the lab and then stabilized. They were not dealing with a simple cemetery excavation; in fact, no one on the team had ever worked on such a site.

Doran and Dickel were terrestrial archaeologists, used to digging in the sandy soils of Texas or the rich loam of California. The pond required a whole new way of thinking: a totally new approach to site preparation, excavation, and conservation.

The edge of the pond during early demucking. Photo courtesy of G. Doran.

As the team assembled at the site, they confronted the logistics of the pond. What to do with all that water? They needed a way to effectively remove the water from the pond so that excavations could proceed, but it wasn't as simple as just draining the pond. The bones were coming from the dense layers of peat at the pond's base; if the pond was drained and the peat allowed to dry out completely, it would crack and slump, making excavations difficult and putting the skeletons at risk. The team needed to be able to drain the pond in a controlled manner — evacuate the water while keeping the peat moist. It required a careful balancing act; one that would take at least the first field season to perfect.

Doran and Dickel turned to Bill Tanner. When it came to construction, Bill had already proven himself a jack-of-all-trades. Swann depended on him to solve the water-removal issue, asking him to take the lead in figuring out the best course of action. Bill assured him he was up to the task; he would devise a system through which the team could control the draining of the pond. The issue was left in Bill's capable hands.

Bill knew just about everything there was to know about construction. He could handle heavy equipment, he could coordinate field crews, and he could lay water lines until the cows came home. Yet who could have anticipated the need to drain a pond to get at skeletons buried beneath? He was stumped.

Bill may not have had all the answers, but what he did have was a vast network of associates within the construction industry. Whatever issues arose in the field, he knew who to call for advice. He first turned to his friend Ollie King. Ollie was a dewatering expert. He had perfected his skills through years of "jacking and boring" under major arterial roads in Florida. Because of Florida's shallow water table, digging in most regions of the state is limited to about four feet before you strike water. Olli advised Bill on possible methods of achieving the proper conditions for excavations and from that point on, Bill took the reigns as Windover's dewatering expert.

Next, Bill contacted Thompson Pumps, a company based in Daytona Beach. Thompson specializes in centrifugal pumps, trash pumps, and complete dewatering systems; anything you would need to get water out of a pond. He had worked with Thompson in the past. He called them and began with, "Now let me give you a scenario." He described the pond, the peat, and the fact that there were archaeologists waiting in the wings. Bill's main concerns were the dense layers of peat they would be working in and the depth of the pond, which would turn out to be deeper than anyone anticipated.

In consultation with Thompson, Bill decided to use three-inch pipes that would reach twenty feet in depth. The pipes would be driven into the ground using a backhoe (enter Steve Vanderjagt); they would be "jetted," meaning the muck and soil would be evacuated from the pipes; and then pumps would be attached to pull water from the pond. But jetting wellpoints within layers of peat was much more complicated than working within normal terrestrial soils. Wellpoints contain tiny slits at their base through which the water is drawn; the peat (muck) would clog the slits, blocking the flow of water. Thus, they

Early stages of excavations, using extensive well points to drain the pond. Photo courtesy of G. Doran.

would need to fill the pipes with "wellpoint sand," special large-grained porous sand that would allow the water to filter through.

The consensus on site was that a large area of the pond, about the size of an Olympic swimming pool, would be sectioned off and drained. This would provide a designated area in which the crews could excavate. A continuous line of dump trucks hauled sand to the pond, depositing it to form earthen walls around the excavation area. Doran and Dickel decided they would start excavations where Steve's backhoe had first encountered skeletons. Wellpoints would be placed within the section to control drainage and the evacuated water would be siphoned off. Problems arose almost immediately.

The earthen walls did little to protect the excavation area. They tended to slump, obstructing excavations and requiring constant maintenance. Storms made the situation even worse, as heavy rains degraded the walls. The depth of the pond was deceiving; the construction crews had assumed it was shallow, like so many of the ponds they had already worked through when constructing Windover Way. But the central portion of the pond, which appeared to produce a steady

Dickel and Doran stand within the drained pond to discuss logistics. Photo courtesy of G. Doran.

seep of groundwater, turned out to be over twenty feet in depth, complicating both the dewatering strategy and future excavations.

While Swann's crews worked on dewatering the pond, Doran and Dickel tested the adjacent hammock, which they believed might hold remnants of living sites. During the early phases of construction, as bulldozers had smoothed the terrain north of the pond by scraping off the top layers of vegetation, large dark stains appeared in the sand. About twelve blackened circles dotted the area, which the crews described as "firepits"—ancient campfires that unfortunately were obliterated by the time Doran and Dickel arrived on scene. Perhaps the hammock held additional clues.

They marked off the hammock in ten-meter grids, "shovel testing" at each point. Shovel tests provide a way for archaeologists to sample a site without conducting full-scale excavations. At each ten-meter mark, a small deep hole is dug. The earth removed is screened, and any artifacts found are collected, bagged, and labeled as to their location on the

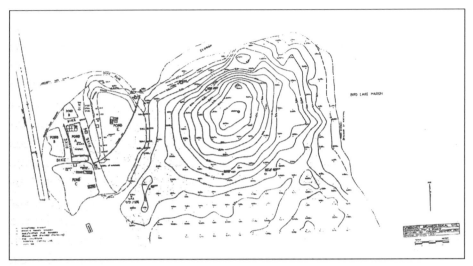

Topographic map of the pond and the adjacent knoll. Photo courtesy of G. Doran.

site. When a shovel test is "positive," the archaeologist may decide to open a "unit," typically a one-meter by one-meter square that provides a broader picture of the area producing artifacts. If large numbers of artifacts are encountered within a unit, it can be expanded; thus archaeologists can focus their work on the productive areas within a site. When shovel testing is complete, the points sampled are mapped and the tests that produced artifacts are highlighted. The highlighted areas reveal distribution patterns throughout a site, indicating where people were living or working by the clusters and types of materials they left behind. But the artifacts recovered from the adjacent hammock proved to be from a much later occupation than the individuals buried in the pond. The first indication was the presence of pottery.

Pottery in Florida first occurred around five thousand years ago and is used as a rough temporal gauge for archaeological sites. Sites without pottery, referred to as pre-ceramic, can be reasonably assumed to predate five thousand years; the presence of pottery indicates later occupations. Once pottery was invented and spread throughout Florida, the pottery's styles and the materials used to produce them changed over time and across geographical regions. The earliest forms of pottery are rough in texture due to the fibers incorporated in the clay. These fiber-tempered ceramics serve as the introduction of pottery among Native Americans in Florida. Around three thousand years ago, early Floridians began to use grit and sand as "tempers" and vessel decorations became more elaborate as methods of production improved. By two thousand years ago, ceramics were "incised" using sharp tools to produce geometrical patterns and intricate lines on vessels. Wooden paddles with small squares carved into their surfaces produced the well-known "check-stamped" vessels of the St. Johns region around one thousand years ago. What began as plain, rough-textured utilitarian vessels evolved into elaborate works of art. Over time, regional cultures throughout the state could be identified by the decorative styles of their pottery. Thus, the presence and style of ceramics are used as "diagnostic" artifacts within archaeological sites. The same can be said about stone points, whose styles evolved over time as techniques improved and hunting strategies shifted to smaller game.

The crews at Windover knew that whoever was living on the hammock came at least several thousand years later than those interred in the pond, since shovel testing produced St. Johns check-stamped pottery. It was the lack of pottery in the spoils that was Doran's first hint of the pond's antiquity.

Once the excavation area within the pond was prepped and the water evacuated, digging commenced. Using his backhoe, Steve would carefully remove layer after layer of the heavy muck, while Doran and Dickel stood nervously by. As soon as the pale bones appeared, Steve would back out of the area and the field crew would move in. What they found was a bit disappointing. The skeletons were a mess. Those interred in that area of the pond had shifted toward the deeper points. The remains were jumbled together and there was little evidence of discrete burials, so vital to archaeological interpretation.

The crews gradually developed the techniques necessary for excavating within the peat. It was not like excavating in terrestrial soils. The peat was more a thick clay-like consistency that had to be sliced instead

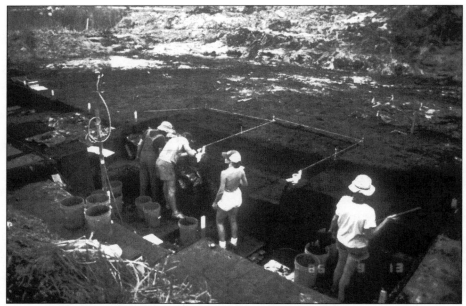

Excavations required strategies adapted to the density of the matrices. Photo courtesy of R. Brunck.

of scraped. Its original red-brown color would quickly transform to black as the peat oxidized once it was exposed to air. It required sharp tools. Trowels and shovels were sharpened to fine blades and wielded with care to avoid injuries. By carefully removing a thin layer of peat with a shovel using long "shovel shaves," the excavators would slowly slice through the muck until the tell-tale change in color or texture of the peat indicating a burial. Switching over to wooden tools so as not to damage the bone, they would carefully scrape the muck away from the bone's surface, working until the entire bone was exposed in place, known as 'pedestalling.' The tools of choice were chopsticks, absconded from nearby Chinese restaurants. By tapering the flat end to a thin wedge and tempering the sticks over the heat from their cook stoves, the chopsticks were made hardened and resilient, the perfect tool for flicking pieces of peat from the bones' delicate surfaces. Each excavator had their own "favorite tool," an implement that was familiar and battle tested. Some used the plastic handles from Dairy Queen

Dickel "pedestalling" a burial before it is mapped, photographed, and then removed. Photo courtesy of R. Brunck.

spoons; others arrived on scene with elaborate excavation kits. Whatever the tool of choice, the main goal was to protect the bones from damage.

One of the best tools was not really a tool at all: water. Excavators kept large plastic spray bottles of water nearby at all times. The water served two purposes: first, when bone was exposed, the water was used to keep the skeletons moist and prevent the drying and cracking that can occur when wet bone is allowed to dry too quickly. The second purpose was to remove peat adhering to the bones. As skeletons emerged from the dark peat, they were repeatedly doused with water until they could be removed from the ground.

The crews were housed within a small cluster of apartments in Cocoa during the first field season. Their days started early. They would load their gear—tool boxes filled with trowels, tape measures, string, assorted brushes, files, flagging tape, waterproof markers, and plastic bags—and drive the twenty minutes north to Titusville. Once there, they would unload their vehicles, take up their assigned places, and get to work. The crews were broken into two teams: the excavators were made up of trained personnel; Dickel oversaw their progress and monitored their work. The other half, many of whom were local volunteers, manned the row of screens where bucket after bucket of muck was hauled, dumped, and rinsed using a web of hoses that snaked beneath their feet. The water forced the mud and muck through the 1/8 inch screens, which caught small bones (both human and faunal) and any artifacts that may have been incorporated with the burials.

A daily routine quickly settled upon the crews. Work would progress throughout the morning until lunch was called. Excavators would pick their way out of the pond, cautiously stepping on the planks of plywood spread out as makeshift stepping stones so as not to sink into the muck or crush the burials. Those at the screens would rinse the earth from their hands, scraping the muck from underneath their fingernails, relishing the coolness of the water. Having spent the morning hunched over a burial, meticulously scraping earth from bone, the excavators would use the break for short walks in the woods to loosen their limbs and ease their cramping muscles.

The crews would gather for lunch on the sandy ridge adjacent to the hammock. Most brought their lunch. Those who didn't piled into one of the battered pickups and drove to the nearby gas station, where they gorged themselves on hot dogs, chips, and sodas. Dickel developed a serious cola addiction during the first field season; each day he mechanically headed to the gas station for his mandatory super-sized soda, the van seemingly driving itself.

Many days in the field ended with a quick trip to the coast, where the excavators would bathe in the warm waters off Canaveral National Seashore. Coated in black peat from head to toe, stiff from the hours spent hovering over a burial or bending over the screens, the crews would plunge into the crashing waves, rinsing the black earth from their bodies. They would then head for their cramped apartments, where they would collect grapefruit that had fallen from the numerous trees encircling their complex or gather for a communal meal of spaghetti and beer.

The initial months were long and hot. August in Florida is a miserable mix of oppressive heat, stifling humidity, and voracious mosquitoes. The sun is relentless, the rhythmic grating call of cicadas deafening. There is no such thing as an Indian summer in Florida. The summer heat persists through September until one miraculous morning you wake up and the air holds that first fresh hint of fall. The humidity evaporates, the skies turn a crystalline blue, and the warm coastal winds are pushed offshore by cooler air from the north.

The work progressed. Days stretched into months as the season slid toward fall and a steady trickle of bones emerged from the pond. But one of the site's most astounding discoveries was just on the horizon.

Shadows in a Skull

It was late in the day and Dickel and one of the volunteers, Billie Barton, were finishing up with an exposure. Most of the crew had already left the site, heading south to drop off the day's skeletons at the lab and return to their small apartments for an early evening. The sun was sliding west and the shadows from the nearby tree line were spreading slowly across the adjacent clearing.

Dickel and Barton were examining a crushed skull that had been exposed earlier in the day. There was something unusual about this skull: not the skull itself, but the mushy smear that lay just beneath the upper surface of bone. It resembled the marl from the rim of the pond —that same smooth consistency, yet subtly different in color and texture. Perhaps it was the remnants of an *endocast*, which forms when the cranial cavity fills with soil that hardens, producing a mass whose surface reflects the contours of the inner vault. Dickel took a small scrap of paper and rubbed a bit of the smear onto it. He watched as it formed a small grease stain: definitely organic, definitely not marl.

Later that evening, Dickel discussed the strange substance with Doran, who joked in his West Texas drawl that perhaps it was just "snail poop." The next day, they removed the skull and placed it in the freezer for safe keeping. Using boiling water, they sterilized a plastic spoon left over from a recent trip to Dairy Queen and carefully scraped a sample of the mushy substance into a sealed container. They sent it off to a lab in Orlando, hoping the lab's high-tech equipment could identify the mysterious substance. But the lab, which specialized in water sampling, could not provide a positive ID. All they could say was that it was definitely organic. So the excavations continued and Doran and Dickel remained suspicious.

Could the strange substance be brain tissue? If so, it wouldn't be the first ancient brain to emerge from a wet site in Florida. Brain tissue had reportedly been recovered from Warm Mineral Springs, a site in southwest Florida that was excavated by an amateur archaeologist and

Remnants of brain matter within one of the skulls. Photo courtesy of G. Doran.

diver, but the material was never positively identified. Could Windover be the real thing?

It wasn't until a more complete skull emerged from the peat that Doran and Dickel were able to get a better look at the strange substance within. And based on the material's shape and characteristic convoluted surface, they knew they had a significant find on their hands; they were definitely dealing with brains. They headed for the phones to call for backup.

Fortunately, Dickel had an inside connection: his wife was an organic biochemist who specialized in cloning DNA. She put them in touch with Alan Wilson, whose team at Berkley had recently cloned ancient DNA extracted from the preserved hide of a quagga, an extinct form of zebra. Wilson directed them to Bill Hauswirth and Phillip Laipis at the University of Florida's Shands Medical Center in Gainesville. Hauswirth and Laipis had been extracting mitochondrial DNA from bovine brain tissue. They happily agreed to work on the brains from Windover, and after several weeks their attempts proved successful. The DNA

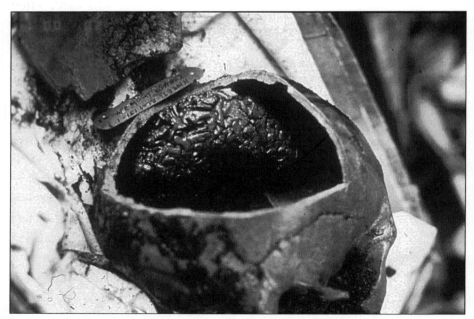

A preserved brain still exhibits its original shape, although somewhat shrunken. Photo courtesy of R. Brunck.

confirmed that the Windover skulls had brains. A sarcastic editorial in the local paper announced, "Brains finally discovered in Titusville!"

By the end of the first field season, several intact brains were recovered. Although shrunken, many retained the shape and surface features of contemporary brain tissue. At the time of its discovery, the brain tissue from Windover represented the most ancient DNA yet analyzed at the molecular level. The better preserved brains had shrunk to about one-quarter their original size and were a mottled tan and grey. As time went on and more brains were recovered, an agreement was drafted between FSU and Wuesthoff Hospital in Rockledge, just south of Cocoa, for storage of the delicate tissues. When a skull containing brain was excavated, it was kept damp and placed in a plastic bag for transport to Wuesthoff, where it was stored in freezers within the Pathology Department, alongside tissue and organ samples extracted from modern patients. The hospital's radiologists were also anxious to assist. The skulls containing brain matter were X-rayed and scanned, the teams working under the cover of nightfall so that imaging of the ancient remains did not interfere with patient care. They were then sent on to Gainesville where Hauswirth and Laipis would continue their attempts at DNA extraction from the fragile tissues.

Molecular analyses have radically improved our ability to trace human lineages through time. By tracking components within deoxyribonucleic acid (DNA), primarily mitochondrial DNA (mtDNA)—passed down through the maternal line, and Y chromosomal DNA—passed down through the paternal line, we can trace the genetic history of humans back over 140,000 years to a common ancestor in Africa. Fast forward 120,000 years and we can use haplogroups, which are genetic sequences shared between related populations, to discern human migration into the Americas. We use these sequences to retrace population histories over time and space, since groups that are related will share these sequences and spread them as populations grow and expand. DNA analysis has confirmed the Asiatic origins of Native Americans. Prior to the advent of DNA analysis, physical resemblances (such as characteristic eye folds we see in live populations and similarities in skull measurements and dental traits we see in skeletal

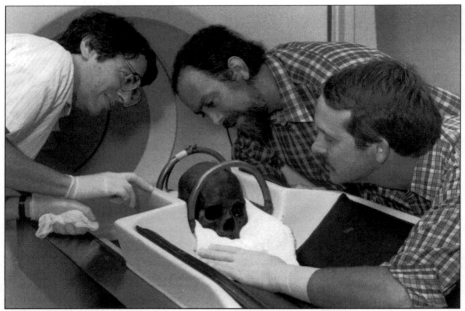

Doran (right) assists in scanning one of the Windover skulls. Photo courtesy of G. Doran.

remains), blood groupings (which served as the first physiological link between Native Americans and Asian populations), and linguistics (using root words in Native American languages to trace their origins) were relied on to infer relatedness between the continents. Yet exactly when they arrived and how they got here (via land migration or using water craft along the western coasts) remains a contentious issue among archaeologists.

The brains also provided clues to Windover burial customs. The tissues lacked gas vacuoles that are produced as decomposition advances; they typically appear within forty-eight hours following death. The fact that the Windover brains lacked these vacuoles indicated that burials within the pond took place within that forty-eight hour window. If the people buried at Windover were living nearby, the first days following the death of the individual were possibly spent performing rituals or preparing the body for interment. If travel to the pond was required, the lack of vacuoles indicates they were living in close enough proximity that they could make the trip within a day or two.

The brains were another intricate piece of what would become an amazing puzzle. The same neutral anaerobic conditions that preserved the bones from Windover also provided the perfect environment for the preservation of the brains. The better preserved the skull, the more likely it was to contain brain tissue. The intact skulls protected the brains in death, just as they had in life.

At Windover, even though elevated sulfur levels within the highly mineralized water of the pond reduced oxidation of the DNA, seven thousand years cannot pass without destruction and breakdown of its delicate components. Analyses that would determine the people of Windover were not related to any living Native American populations or any prehistoric groups yet sampled, would come several decades later, not from the brain tissue but from DNA extracted from fragments of the well-preserved bones. Although the people of Windover carry genetic markers that link them to ancient populations from Asia, they do not match native populations alive in North America today. Either their descendants died off or their numbers were drastically reduced at some point prior to the evolution of the genetic markers we see in modern populations. Either way, their genetic history remains a mystery that awaits the advancement of technology before it is fully illuminated.

The discovery of brains became a fantastic closing act for the first field season. It brought the site national media attention, which only intensified as each new discovery was made. As the three-month season was winding down, Doran and Dickel began planning for next year. They would need money, which required another round with the Florida legislature; they would need man power, which they had in abundance, especially as word of the excavation and local interest in the site spread; and they would need a better dewatering strategy.

Back at the lab, the bones were stabilized, catalogued, and prepared for transport to Florida State. There were about thirty-two individuals recovered, nine of them children. Most were recovered from the spoils and were represented by isolated bones. The individuals from the base of the pond were mostly commingled with few complete skeletons among them. Doran and Dickel hoped the next field season would provide more complete burials from which they could investigate this most unusual style of burial.

SECTION TWO

FLORIDA'S ANCIENT POND CEMETERIES

As unique a site as Windover was at the time of its discovery, it wasn't the first mortuary pond discovered in Florida. Apparently, this style of interment was practiced by other Archaic Period populations thousands of years ago, for Windover was the fifth of such sites to emerge from Florida's ancient past.

The first two mortuary ponds to be investigated were not actually ponds but springs. Located in Sarasota County, Warm Mineral Springs is a site made famous for the curative properties of its warm, highly mineralized waters. Also located in Sarasota County, about three kilometers away, is Little Salt Springs (for some reason both site names are pluralized, even though they are singular springs). Both sites were investigated in the 1950s by amateur archaeologist and diver Bill Royal, who recovered human remains from the periphery of each spring's conical base. Warm Mineral Springs made headlines for its highly publicized (though speculative) recovery of a human skull containing remnants of brain tissue during the taping of a documentary on the site. The skull was recovered from a ledge within the spring as a nearby camera captured the action. Some claimed Royal had staged the recovery for dramatic effect. The camera then followed the collectors to a lab where the skull was dramatically cut open, as chunks of convoluted tissue spilled onto the examining table. A neurosurgeon confirmed that the pieces of tissue appeared to be human brain and the presence of cholesterol was confirmed by a biochemist, yet the discovery predated our modern techniques of DNA analysis and no follow-up has ever been reported. Only seven individuals were recovered from Warm Mineral Springs, none represented by complete skeletons.

Royal also collected at Little Salt Springs, plucking remains representing over forty individuals from the base of the spring and bringing them to the surface in laundry baskets. Some of the remains were later displayed in his home, where they were mortared into his fireplace

51

hearth. Because the recovery of remains from both springs was not carried out by professionally trained archaeologists and therefore lacks the important information concerning their provenience within the springs, much of the crucial information concerning the mortuary practices surrounding them has been lost.

The next mortuary pond, Republic Groves, was discovered in Hardee County in the late 1960s. In order to prepare the ground for the planting of a citrus grove, construction crews were attempting to fill in a swampy area and two small adjacent springs with surface peat scraped from the area. After several failed attempts, they began carving canals through the soft peats when they noticed human remains, animal bones, and artifacts emerging from the spoils being thrown up along the periphery of the canals. Salvage excavations were undertaken to collect the materials, but, like Warm Mineral and Little Salt, provenience was hampered not by collection methods but because the site had already been completely disturbed by the construction crews. The remains they were able to recover represented around thirty-seven individuals, but there were no complete skeletons, simply isolated bones.

The final mortuary pond to be discovered prior to Windover was Bay West. The Bay West Nursery, located in Collier County, was dredging a cypress pond for use as a water source and to mine the rich peat at its base for fertilizer when human remains appeared in the spoil piles. The bones were deemed ancient by local law enforcement and construction continued. A local anthropological group conducted salvage excavations in conjunction with the dredging operations and was able to collect the poorly preserved bones and associated artifacts coming from the pond's base. The bones represented over thirty-five people, but their fragmented nature and the lack of provenience minimized the archaeological potential of the site. The excavations at Windover would represent the only properly controlled fieldwork conducted within any of the pond cemeteries yet discovered in Florida.

Had any of these sites been discovered today, laws that have been put in place over the last twenty years that prohibit the disturbance of human remains, whether the graves are ancient or modern, would have protected the sites from further destruction. Under Chapter 872.05 of Florida Statutes, all human remains are accorded equal treatment and it is a third degree felony to knowingly disturb a grave, a second degree felony not to report a known offense.

Florida's five mortuary ponds are most likely a small sampling of this style of interment that was practiced during the Archaic period. We don't know how many other ponds or springs served as cemeteries. How many other small bodies of water are out there holding clues to Florida's ancient peoples?

Demucking, Part Two

The remains excavated during the first field season were analyzed by Dickel during the spring, while Doran worked on the proposal requesting another year's worth of funding from the legislature. The request was approved and $240,000 was granted for the second field season.

As the summer of 1985 churned on, Doran and Dickel prepared for the next season by addressing the dewatering strategy. The first season's strategy wouldn't do; they needed a better means of controlling the water within the pond and they needed a larger area in which to work. They worked with Tanner and Swann to devise a solution.

Instead of cordoning off a small area of the pond, which was marred with complications of maintaining the earthen walls, they decided that the next field season would see the entire pond drained. That way, they

Excavations in progress: the green pickle buckets were used to remove surrounding soils from the burials. Photo courtesy of R. Brunck.

54

could expand their excavation areas on a broader scale, hopefully striking intact burials instead of the disarticulated, jumbled remains of the first season. They would add additional wellpoints to manage the enlarged area and leave the wells in place between the second and third season, with Swann graciously agreeing to cover the cost of leasing the equipment throughout the year. With the wells left in place, setup would be minimized for the third season; all they would have to do is hook up the large diameter hose, attach the pumps, and commence drainage.

It worked like a charm. The additional wellpoints provided greater control throughout the pond, and the field crews could expand their excavations. They would target two areas within pond: the first on the east side of the pond, the second to the southwest, directly south of the first year's excavation. They hoped to encounter greater burial densities in these new areas and anticipated that the burials in these shallower regions might be more intact. The areas would turn out to be similar to the original excavation area: the eastern unit would produce only one individual, a juvenile; the southwest unit would prove a bit more productive.

Back at the Lab

Another issue that needed to be revisited was the conservation of the bones. When Doran and Dickel first visited the site and realized they were dealing with remains and artifacts from a wet site, they knew they would have to devise a special strategy for the conservation of each item that came out of the pond. Doran spent the following months combing the literature for conservation strategies to employ at Windover.

During the first season, when remains were removed from the pond, they were rinsed with water, placed in sealed plastic bags for transport to the lab where they were transferred to large, black vats of "consolidant." A consolidant is a special mixture of adhesive used for the preservation of fragile archaeological specimens, including bone, ceramics, paper—anything requiring stabilization. It comes in several forms, from tubes of thick glue-like substances to liquids diluted with water, depending on the material on which it will be used. It is diluted to achieve the desired consistency and applied directly to the artifact or bones or prepared in tubs in which items are placed to soak. Once the material has absorbed enough of the mixture to be considered stable (typically when absorption has ceased), the item is removed and allowed to dry.

They used polyethylene glycol (PEG) during the first field season. When the bones arrived at the lab, they were removed from their plastic bags and placed directly into vats of PEG solution, which was mixed with water, alcohol, and a fungicide to prevent mold. The bones would soak in their baths until enough of the solution had penetrated the tissues, restoring their strength and hardness and preventing further deterioration and cracking. The problem with PEG was the size of its molecules: its large molecules required weeks, if not months, to penetrate the cellular structure of the bones. During that time, the remains were checked for mold and the water chemistry was monitored. The skeletons sat in their vats for weeks on end, as the concentration of PEG was slowly increased until the bone tissue was fully saturated and absorption of the PEG had ceased. The larger the bone, the longer the soak; femurs could take over a month. This lengthy process was cumbersome; as more bones emerged from the pond, the lab became glutted with the large black vats. The bones under treatment at the end of the first season had to be carefully transported via U-Haul the three hundred miles from Titusville to Tallahassee in their PEG baths, a most tenuous process. They needed a more expedient means of stabilizing the remains.

They turned to Roplex, an acrylic emulsion whose smaller molecules penetrated the bones in fifteen or twenty minutes versus the lengthy treatments associated with PEG. The process was similar to PEG: the bones arrived in the lab and were removed from the plastic bags, placed immediately into the Roplex bath for a brief soak, and then

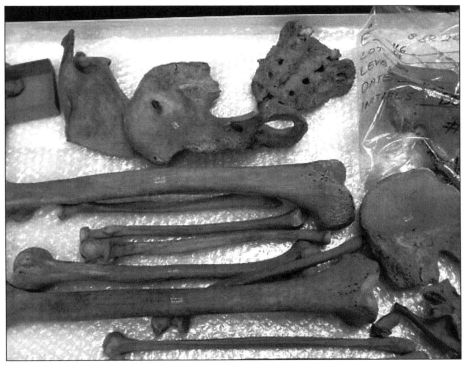

One of the well-preserved skeletons. Photo courtesy of G. Doran.

Many of the skulls were highly fragmented, crushed from the weight of surrounding soils. Photo courtesy of G. Doran.

removed and left to dry on racks. The lab crew could work through a number of bones per day, a vast improvement over the PEG process. The only precaution was the acidic nature of the Roplex. If the bones were left in the bath too long, the acidity of the Roplex would begin to break down the skeletal tissues and dissolve the bones; thus, careful monitoring was required. Bones would go into the bath and the timer would start. Once time was up, the bones were removed and the lab crews would move on to the next batch. The lab worked like a well-oiled Roplex machine.

The different processes (PEG versus Roplex) produced different bone consistencies. The PEG-treated bones turned a dark brown and were waxy to the touch; those bathed in Roplex were unaltered by the treatment, their surfaces clean and dry. Certain bones were set aside for molecular analysis, since conservation treatments can hamper the extraction of DNA and stable isotopes. Fragments of rib or chunks of longbone shafts were ideal for molecular analyses and therefore they bypassed the baths and went directly into the freezer. Teeth are also ideal candidates for such analyses because of the self-contained nature of the enamel and the fact that teeth, unlike bones, do not remodel over time (meaning they remain unchanged from the time they develop in the jaws). They were treated no differently than bone. Jaws containing teeth were bathed in Roplex, as were isolated teeth recovered from nearby skulls.

Crushed skulls presented greater problems. Some of the crania arrived at the lab in small pieces, especially the more fragile skulls of the children. Time and pressure reduced many of the skulls to shattered bits, requiring patient, meticulous reconstruction by Dickel and his crew. The fragments were first treated with Roplex, allowed to dry, then carefully put back together like three-dimensional jigsaw puzzles. It took a delicate touch, a precise eye, and hours of tedious labor, turning pieces over and over in one's hands to identify the jagged edges that fit together. By matching pieces, one by one, the skulls slowly took shape. Some came together quickly; those in larger fragments with fewer pieces to reconstruct. Some were in pieces the size of fingernails, requiring days and sometimes weeks to complete.

Dickel and staff would have four or five skulls going at once. Using highly concentrated Roplex (as well as B72, another acrylic emulsion adhesive), they would glue a piece to a skull, hold it in place until it began to set, and then carefully put the skull down to dry, usually in a small container filled with sand. The sand provided a soft surface that would conform to the shape and curvature of the skull, a perfect resting place as the glue set. They would then move on to the next skull, and the next, and the next. Eventually, the skulls that arrived in pieces were restored to their original shape, traces of their former condition visible as faint scars on their surfaces.

Conservation has developed into a highly specialized discipline. Conservationists work within museums, art galleries, and auction houses, stabilizing and reconstructing artifacts and works of art recovered from around the world. Their skills depend on adhesives and restoration products especially designed for the delicate materials on which

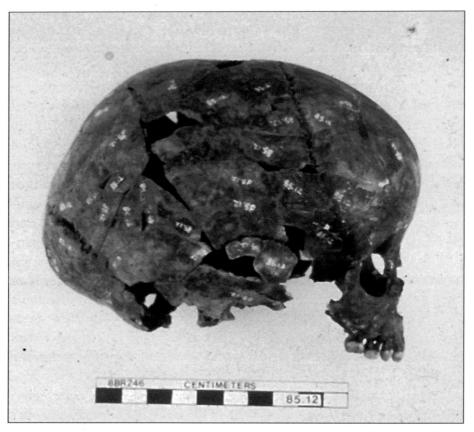

A reconstructed cranium of a child. Over half the burials were those of children. Photo courtesy of R. Brunck.

they work, including bone. Gone are the days when archaeologists would try any means of gluing together fragmented remains. Once-shattered bones still line the shelves of dusty museum cabinets, held together using such inventive materials as Elmer's glue or Duco cement. Today's high-tech consolidants are chemically designed for conservation and produce a more refined finished product; no more flaking paste or crumbling bonds, a favorite meal of rodents and bugs, who seem to love the crispy residue of out-dated adhesives.

By the second year, Dickel had become a permanent resident in Titusville; his wife joined him during the second season, relocating to

Gainesville to work with Hauswirth and Laipis at Shands. Between field seasons, he would toil away in the lab, conserving remains, reconstructing skulls, and collecting information from the bones. Each element that entered the lab was carefully labeled with a unique number. If an element was in pieces, each piece was labeled. You can imagine the intricate work required for the shattered skulls, with every small fragment requiring the burial number from which it came.

Commingled burials were even more problematic. When multiple individuals are clustered within a single grave (which occurred frequently at Windover in the deeper portions of the pond where bodies had shifted over time), the bodies must be separated into discrete individuals so that analyses such as determining the age, sex, height, and physical dimensions of the individual can be obtained. It is this valuable information that provides the "demographics" or population structure of a cemetery. When commingled burials involve people of different age and sex, it can be relatively easy to distinguish individuals based on the size and robusticity of their bones. A young adult male skeleton is easily distinguishable from an older female skeleton. Males tend to be taller and more robust, and they display physical traits (especially on the skull) that easily identify them as "male," such as a square jaw, prominent brow ridge, and larger muscle attachment sites. Females tend to be more "gracile" or lightly built, are generally smaller (both in height and general size of their bones), and display obvious traits of the female sex, such as a wider pelvis and less robust skulls.

When jumbled burials involve individuals of similar age, "sexing" the skeletons can at least break the group into two camps: male and female. Dealing with the elderly and the young is a bit more complicated.

As our skeletons age strange things happen. Aside from the onslaught of arthritis, fractures, and osteoporosis, the traits that make "sexing" the skeleton in adults fairly straightforward diminish as an individual ages. Older male skeletons can appear more "feminine"; elderly females can become more "masculine." These changes are especially true of the skull. The angles and landmarks typical of a younger male's jaw and skull may diminish; as they lose muscle mass, their skeletons can become less robust. The jaws of elderly females can become more angular as they age and can be confused with those of males. This "switching" makes sexing an elderly skeleton challenging, especially among incomplete remains when you must rely on fragmented skeletons for analysis.

Especially difficult are commingled juveniles. Children's skeletons do not display the physical characteristics typical of their sex until after puberty, when increases in testosterone and progesterone cause the skeleton to morph into the shapes and dimensions representative of their sex. The skulls of young males become more masculine, their bones more robust; the pelves of females take on the wide, bowl shape necessary for childbirth. In commingled burials of children, where sex cannot be determined, distinguishing individuals of similar ages can be difficult, if not impossible. The skeleton of a ten-year-old boy can be indistinguishable from that of a ten-year-old girl. Since females' physical maturation takes place earlier in life, it can be easy to mistake the skeletons of girls for those of boys (picture a grade school class photo, with many of the girls towering over the shorter males!). Unless you are fortunate enough to obtain (and have the funding to pay for) DNA for analysis, sexing juvenile skeletons cannot be done reliably. Through DNA we can examine the child's sex chromosomes: X for females, Y for males. At Windover it would be too challenging and too costly to try to extract DNA from each of the children in order to determine their sex, especially since half the burials eventually recovered would be individuals who never made it to adulthood.

The work being performed in the lab was focused on preserving the remains and accurately cataloguing each item that came out of the pond. One of the individuals tasked with this job was Vera Zimmerman. Like many of the volunteers who brought their own set of skills and talents to the project, Vera was well-suited for the tedious work of cataloguing. One of her greatest gifts was her eyesight (or lack thereof): Vera was extremely nearsighted, which proved highly beneficial when having to write very small numbers on tiny fragments of bone. She could work for hours on end, documenting in tiny white letters the burial numbers for each bit of bone that came across her table. But it was her background that really suited her for work at Windover.

Vera was a native Louisianan, born and raised in New Orleans, where she developed a love for art and history. She attended college at the University of Houston, where she majored in art. Needing to fill additional course requirements, she checked off a number of courses that caught her eye in the college catalogue, all of which were in anthropology. Her advisor recommended a double major, which she completed in 1976. You could say her interest in anthropology was deeply rooted.

Vera was a fifth generation native of Louisiana and had always been intrigued with tracing her ancestry. Her years of genealogical research proved fruitful; her connection to Native Americans lay several hundred years in her family's past. A distant uncle, a farmer who had relocated to Massachusetts, was killed during the 1675 Native American uprising known as King Phillip's War. He was slain in his field by Native Americans caught up in the revolt led by Metacomet (known to the English as King Phillip), who directed the uprising against the English colonists that resulted in the destruction of almost half the colonies and many dead Englishmen, her uncle among them.

Another of her relatives was a bit more fortunate. A distant aunt was one of thirteen lucky survivors of the Natchez Massacre, which began on November 28, 1729, at nine a.m. on a Monday. A large band of Natchez Indians attacked a French colony, killing 229 people, many of them women and children. Vera's aunt was held captive for over a month while negotiations with the army dragged on. Her aunt's husband wasn't so lucky; he was one of the 229.

Vera and her husband moved to the Cocoa area in 1977, following the completion of her degree. She volunteered at the nearby Brevard Museum of History and Science, serving as co-curator of history. She also joined the local chapter of the Florida Anthropological Society, known as the Indian River Anthropological Society (IRAS). It was as an IRAS member that she first came to the Windover site. In January 1983 the group was tasked with collecting the bones poking from the spoil piles following the demucking that led to the site's discovery. She was among the first to lay her hands on the beautiful remains from Windover.

She worked in the lab during the second and third field season, applying her delicate penmanship to each bone's surface. Her work didn't stop there. She assisted Dickel with making molds of some of the items recovered from the graves with materials she appropriated from her dentist. She was one of over thirty volunteers who tirelessly worked at Windover in some capacity or another. When not in the lab, she led tours for school groups and the public, herding them through the site and providing a running monologue about the excavation's progress.

But one of her most relevant contributions came when they decided to hold an art contest for local artists whose work focused on the excavations. The contest, hosted by the Brevard Artist's Association, included about thirty local artists who were given access to the site to complete sketchings or to take photos from which to work. Vera not only helped arrange the contest, but also competed in it, producing an intricate sketch of Doran at work on the site. When the picture was turned upside down, it was transformed into the sketch of a Native American beside the pond. The artists were given about a month to produce their representative works, which were then put on display at the Brevard Art Museum in Melbourne. Dickel was to serve as judge, much to his dismay since his studies in archaeology and skeletal biology had left little room for art appreciation. Watercolors, charcoal sketches, and photographs adorned the walls of the museum, all of them capturing aspects of the excavations as seen through the artist's eyes. The contest was a huge success and only increased public attention on the site. One of the works, a beautiful painting in pale pastels of a scattering of buckets at the base of the pond, now hangs in Jim Swann's conference room.

The meticulous cataloguing of remains, in conjunction with their location within the pond, would provide Dickel with information necessary to reconstruct the burial sequences at Windover. He would also be able to map out the distribution of burials in the pond and their relationship to one another. Once all the burials were excavated, this information would enable a "mortuary analysis" of the site, which provided a broad picture of the pond's use as a cemetery: where individuals were buried, how they were positioned, what materials were buried with them, and any patterns within the pond. A necessary component for reconstructing the interment history of the pond, as well as an integral part of the documentation of the site, would be photographs of the burials in place. This is where Richard Brunck came in.

Skeletons in Pictures

As a child, Richard never imagined he would one day be photographing seven-thousand-year-old skeletons, although he grew up with an interest in anthropology. He and his brother spent afternoons combing for artifacts among the woods near his home in Sayler Park, Ohio, a small suburb just outside of Cincinnati. His interest in photography originated the early 1970s, after his brother was sent to fight in Vietnam and started sending home pictures of the landscape and its people. Richard soon developed his own interest in photography, saving money he earned from his paper route and sending it overseas to his brother, who purchased a 35-mm Mamiya Sekor camera from the PX in Saigon for him. From that point on Richard was hooked.

His childhood had been a rambling one. His father was an engineer who oversaw transportation of petroleum goods; the family moved about every other year. As Richard matured, so did his photography. He worked his way through the usual subjects, photographing sunsets, landscapes, and trees. He also shot pictures for his high school yearbook. He completed his BA in English with a minor in Art (photography) from the University of Central Florida and went on for his graduate work at FSU. After graduating with an MA in Fine Arts, he stayed on as adjunct faculty, teaching courses within the art department. That was when he heard about a couple of archaeologists in the anthropology department in need of a good photographer. Richard answered their call.

He was brought on board to photograph artifacts and skeletal material in the lab on FSU's campus in the spring of 1985, following the first field season. Doran and Dickel were so impressed with his work that they invited him to join them on site the following August. Richard accepted immediately. Before he knew it, he was packing his bags and heading for Titusville.

His initiation into the field crew was immediate. Each morning before sunrise, he would pack up his two 35-mm Nikon cameras: one loaded with Ektachrome color transparency film, the other with high resolution black and white. He would use both types of film on the burials. Color was important, since it brought out surface details of the skeletons, whose coloring was unique due to their exceptional preservation in the pond. It also came in handy when photographing the layers of peat, since they varied between black and red, depending on their age and composition. The black and white photos would be used for publication; the high resolution would enable enlargements of the photos without sacrificing clarity. Using an old Kaypro computer, he developed a database for the numerous photos he shot. Each photo had to be identified and associated with its respective burial so they could be referenced later. Richard also captured broader aspects of the site. Each morning, he would shoot pictures from the four corners of the excavation; he would repeat the process each evening, when work was completed, thus providing daily documentation of the site's progress.

When not behind his camera, he was put to work like any other member of the team. Most of his peripheral duties were administrative in nature, but Doran and Dickel weren't above putting anyone to work toting peat from the burials to the screens. Richard did his fair share of bucket work.

In the afternoons, when the crews would head to the beach, he would drive along the dykes within Canaveral National Seashore, spotting numerous species of birds that inhabited the area. With diving osprey searching for prey, roseate spoonbills shuffling through the muddy flats, scores of ibis—both white and glossy, sailing above his head—the Seashore was the ideal spot for a bird-loving photographer.

At the site, when a burial was exposed and pedestalled, Dickel would send word for Richard to report, camera and tripod in hand, and begin setup to photograph the remains. A north arrow was placed in the appropriate direction next to the skeleton, as was a small board containing the burial information and a meter stick for scale. Next, he would position his tripod so as to capture the entire image in both color and black and white. He "bracketed" the photos: each shot was cap-

67

tured at normal exposure, then both under- and over-exposed to insure he got the necessary detail. As he shot, an assistant would hold a "diffuse device" in place, a panel of material used to block out the sun and provide the necessary shade for the picture. For each burial, he would snap about eighteen pictures, hoping to capture it in its entirety. At the end of each week, he would send off the color film for processing, and he'd take the black and white film to an off-site dark room where he'd develop it himself.

Working at the Windover site brought many unique opportunities. He captured aerial images from a plane, a crane, and a fire truck; he photographed visiting dignitaries, politicians, and astronauts. He even got to photograph the brains as they came out of the ground. In deference to the brains, he dressed up as one for the annual Halloween party that was held in the clubhouse of their small apartment complex.

Since Windover, Richard has worked on other scientific projects. He travelled with Dr. Mary Pohl, a cultural anthropologist at FSU, to a site called La Venta in Mexico, where he photographed jade works that displayed carefully crafted alphabetical characters. He also took photos for researchers within FSU's Neuroscience Department (then called Psychobiology), as well as additional lab photography for Doran. Windover opened up a new window of opportunity for Richard. He would forever remember his time at the site as "some of the best times of my life."

A beautifully pedestalled burial, meticulously excavated by the crew. Photo courtesy of R. Brunck.

Controlling the Message

The second season of digging was underway, but something had to be done about the media. Since the discovery of the brains, media attention of the site had spread worldwide. Doran was fielding several phone calls a day, all from reporters anxious to hear the story of the site's discovery and progress. He soon discovered that repeating the same account numerous times a day was quickly eating up all his time. They needed help; they needed a professional public relations person.

Doran's wife, Barbara, worked as a communications specialist in Tallahassee. During the first season, she coordinated a press conference so that the media could interview all parties involved in the excavations: the personnel from EKS, Inc.; Doran and Dickel; and Hauswirth and Laipis, who were by then hard at work on the brain tissues. But as the press conference progressed, they quickly realized they needed a designated individual to handle the constant flow of questions. They needed to manage the media more efficiently and free up time to focus on the excavations, but they didn't want to miss out on the opportunity to educate the public about the significance of archaeological sites in Florida, using Windover as a prime example. They also wanted to highlight the role EKS had played in the site's discovery, focusing on the firm's willingness to facilitate excavations and the impact their financial assistance was having on the field work.

At the time of the site's discovery, public archaeology was in its infancy. The deliberate involvement of the public was typically not a factor when fieldwork was planned. Most archaeological projects are conducted by university faculty or government organizations, with little interaction with the public. The technical articles produced by faculty researchers are published in academic journals and usually read only by fellow academics. Government agencies produce dry reports that are filed away within their vast catalogues, to be unearthed years later, if at all.

The need for archaeologists to engage the public was becoming a vital aspect in obtaining public support and cooperation in the protection of sites throughout the state. Doran saw Windover as the perfect opportunity to publicize the site's depth of history and its significance in understanding prehistoric populations in Florida. Engaging the public was easy: the number of well-preserved bones coming from the pond, the fact that the pond was used as a cemetery and the discovery of seven-thousand-year-old brains was more than enough to hold the public's attention; that the public could actually watch excavations in action was simply icing on the cake. Visitors increased as time went on, with the numbers jumping after news of the brains made national headlines.

Doran decided to apportion part of his funds to hire a full-time communications specialist. Madeleine Carr was perfect for the job.

Madeleine describes herself as "an Anglo-Swiss American." She was born in Surrey, England, to a Swiss father and English mother. Her voice is light and rhythmic, her "o"s beautifully rounded. She speaks with soft British inflections that hint of her childhood migration from England to Switzerland; she was five years old when her father relocated the family to Zurich. When I asked her how she ended up in the United States, she replied, "Otis Redding."

While in college in Switzerland, Madeleine was drawn into the world of jazz. She began as an aficionado, later applying her logistical skills to the organization of large-scale amateur jazz festivals. She had moved back to London at the age of twenty-one, where she worked for the National Jazz Federation. European jazz was undergoing a transformation, morphing into rhythm and blues, much of it coming from the States. She worked under the manager for the Rolling Stones and the Yard Birds, among other leading artists; the job was her first introduction to "long-haired rock musicians."

She and her colleagues later started a PR firm called *Paragon Publicity and Public Relations* and hooked up with Polydor Records, a company who was celebrating their fiftieth anniversary by hosting giant jazz festivals around the world. Madeleine managed one of the largest of these events, the Golden Rose Festival, a three-day lake-side jazz

71

festival in Montreux, Switzerland, celebrating the best of European jazz, but also including such American favorites as Jimi Hendrix. The next year, her firm took the entire London production of the musical *Hair* to Switzerland, where they were forced to invite the Chief of Police because of the show's brief nude scene.

Madeleine knew how to organize. Her work in public and press relations required her to develop a keen adaptability; an "anything goes" attitude where one had to anticipate whatever questions and issues might arise. Her weeks revolved around press receptions. Then Otis Redding died.

Otis Redding was killed on December 10, 1967, when the plane he and his five band members were flying in crashed into the cold waters of Lake Minona on their way to a show in Madison, Wisconsin. Redding was twenty-six years old. One month later, his hit "(Sittin' on) The Dock of the Bay" was released, selling over four million copies. At the time of his death, he was already a star in Europe, bigger even than Elvis Presley. Madeleine's group was charged with putting together the press information, covering his life and musical history. Following Otis's death, his manager, Phil Walden, formed his own record company, Capricorn Records, in Macon, Georgia. By this time, Madeleine had left London and returned to Zurich. In 1970, Madeleine arrived "as an illegal alien with two suitcases" in the small town of Macon to handle PR work for Walden's company. The culture shock was immediate. From Zurich to Macon was too much of a transformation, and she found the work environment "misogynistic." Broke and unable to return to Europe, she convinced the editor of the Macon Telegraph and News that she could write and was hired. She went on to design and develop the paper's entertainment section, which she initiated with record reviews. She met the man she would marry, eventually relocating to Tallahassee, where she went to work for the Division of Tourism. She applied her PR skills to Florida's booming tourist industry, spearheading international tourism for the state. She's lived here ever since. Thus, her love of jazz and the death of a young artist laid a path that would eventually plop Madeleine into the seat of one of the most fantastic archaeological finds of the century.

Madeleine had met Doran's wife, Barbara, at a "Women of Communications" quarterly meeting. When Doran decided to employ a full-time press person, Barbara recommended Madeleine, who had recently left her job with the state to go back to school. She was contemplating a degree in nutrition when Barbara's call came.

Madeleine knew nothing about archaeology. When she sat down with Doran and Dickel at a small Greek restaurant near FSU's campus to discuss the job, things did not go smoothly. Dickel was not on board with hiring a full-time PR person. All he cared about were the excavations; everything else was a distraction. Doran, desperately needing relief from the media, pressed on. Madeleine's lack of archaeological knowledge only added to Dickel's unease. When she started asking questions about the site, miscommunications arose immediately. Madeleine, like all Europeans, is used to thinking in terms of the cultural periods used in her region of the world. "Stone Age," "Bronze Age," and "Iron Age" are familiar terms in Europe. Not so in America. American archaeology uses different terminology, since metallurgy was introduced to most of North America only after European contact. In America the terms "Paleoindian," "Archaic," "Woodland," and "Mississippian" are used to define variation in cultural periods. Doran and Dickel had to translate the American terminology in terms she could understand. Windover was definitely "stone age" in culture, since they lacked metal, but the site post-dated most Stone Age cultures in Europe. It was a bit confusing, to say the least.

Doran's priority was to have Madeleine handle all media inquiries and manage the stream of information coming from the site as excavations proceeded. He wanted to be free from answering the same questions over and over, telling the story of the site's discovery again and again. He needed to focus on broader logistics. Madeleine knew how to deal with the media, but she didn't know anything about Native Americans. She hit the books immediately. She could field questions only if she knew all the answers. She was a pro at shaping a message, reducing complex information to manageable morsels of info that the press and public could comprehend. She had a lot of work ahead.

The entire crew was scheduled to leave for the site over the upcoming Labor Day weekend. Mother Nature had other plans. The 1985 hurricane season, which, like every season began on June 1 and ran through November 30, would be the most active in the United States since 1916, with eight tropical cyclones making landfall, six as full-blown hurricanes. The overall tab for the season would come to over $4 billion with over 240 dead in its wake. Hurricane Elena, who formed off the southern coast of Cuba in late August, slowly made her way into the Gulf of Mexico, where she quickly strengthened, stalled, then strengthened to a category three hurricane, with winds screaming over 115 miles an hour, before slamming into Biloxi, Mississippi, that Labor Day weekend.

Departure was put on hold as crews either fled their coastal residences or hunkered down inland, waiting for Elena to weaken and slide north. After a few days of cleanup, the group reassembled and loaded up for the four-hour trip east.

They arrived in Titusville, settling into their small apartments and preparing their gear for the new season. Shovels and trowels were sharpened; screens were repaired, their screws tightened; and the group's excited chatter reached a crescendo the night before digging commenced.

On the first day of field work, Doran took Madeleine around the site, discussing its logistics and orienting her to the crews, the machinery, and the site's layout. She quickly acclimated to her surroundings as her organizational skills kicked into high gear. She made notes of issues needing to be addressed, scratching out a lengthy list on a yellow legal pad. The construction trailer that would serve as field office had not yet arrived, so she worked while stepping cautiously through the site or sitting under nearby shade trees.

Madeleine's orientation did not end in the field. Her roommate, Tammy Stone, a graduate student who would be overseeing the lab, tutored her during the first season. Evenings in their cramped room were spent in consultation. They would discuss archaeology, anthropology, and all aspects of the excavation. Tammy's mentoring greatly

Media attention grew with each new burial discovered. Photo courtesy of G. Doran.

enhanced Madeleine's education, expediting her introduction to American archaeology.

Madeleine's job quickly swelled beyond PR. She assumed many administrative duties, organizing the delivery of equipment to the field, filing the masses of paperwork that accompanied the grant funds, and handling the details of day-to-day field work. She spent the first season acclimating to the grind of excavations and the flow of information that came with each week of work. The press wanted details: how many bones had been found? How many brains? What kind of artifacts were turning up and what did the burials in the pond signify? The questions never stopped; neither did news from the site. Each week brought more bones, more brains, a spattering of artifacts, and more intriguing hints as to the site's deep history.

The first season had been a PR bonanza. The site's discovery, the commencement of excavations, and the discovery of the brains made for tremendous press. The second season was more subdued.

Excavations reveal the dark layers of peat that held the remains. Photo courtesy of R. Brunck.

Brains continued to be found among many of the skulls but the skeletons themselves were still proving a bit disappointing. The discrete graves Doran and Dickel had hoped for continued to elude them. The bones coming from the new areas were similar to those from the first season: jumbled graves or isolated finds. The intense pace of field work continued throughout the season. The dense layers of peat were slowly peeled away to reveal well-preserved bones similar to the first season. Bones came out of the ground, were shuttled to the lab, preserved, and then readied for transport to FSU. The brains were tucked in the freezers of Weusthoff's pathology department until the end of the season; then they would be shuttled to Gainesville, where the team at Shands would painstakingly extract the delicate strands of DNA from their tissues.

Once funding for the third season was secured, Madeleine's planning began. First, she would address the safety of the site. Safety meant keeping the public out and the skeletons in: they needed a fence. From the time of discovery, the site had been left open and unsecured. As news of Windover spread, visitor traffic increased. On some mornings, as excavators made their way out onto the site to resume work on burials begun the day before, they would see footprints in the peat where nightly visitors had picked their way through the site. The fence was a priority.

Even with funding from the legislature, money was always in short supply. One way to raise funds would be through the sale of tee shirts. Now, visitors could take home a bit of memorabilia, proof they had been to one of the most important archaeological sites in the country. The shirts were a hit and sales went through the roof.

Public education was one of their main priorities. Doran was determined to use the site to promote archaeology and the preservation of sites in Florida, but this had to be done in a controlled manner. The first thing Madeleine wanted to do was shift their Monday-Friday work schedule to Tuesday-Saturday. That way, Fridays could be designated for school group visits and Saturdays for the public, when more people were off from work and able to come out and see the site. To facilitate school visits, Madeleine sent out informationals throughout the local school districts so that teachers wishing to bring their students to the site had to coordinate their visits through her, instead of simply showing up on any day and time. She promoted her program, "Have Lunch with an Archaeologist," where schools could schedule a Friday visit for students to take a tour of the site, return to an area was set up with educational displays, and end their day chatting over sack lunches with a member of the field crew. The students would sit in a circle, wide-eyed and munching on sandwiches, while one of the excavators explained their latest finds. The lunches were a big hit and a unique opportunity for the children.

When the public visited the site, they were no longer allowed to wander the site unchaperoned; the third season would have structure. There would be designated areas, marked off with flagging tape, where the public could walk, ushered along by volunteers. The volunteers came from all walks of life. They didn't care what they did on the site; they just wanted to be a part of the action. Madeleine decided to assign

"Public Days" allowed a first-hand glimpse into the excavations. Photo courtesy of R. Brunck.

each volunteer a subject related to the site. One would learn about core sampling, another about water screening for botanical remains. The volunteer would become well-versed in the subject, able to serve as an information point along the visitor's path. These "human pillars of information" would be strategically placed throughout the site. As visitors made their way along the path, they would stop in front of the "pillar" and be given a brief spiel on a particular subject. With the path in place, the public would be kept on the periphery of the excavations.

The more rigid schedule meant the crews could work undisturbed Tuesday through Thursday, schools could come on Fridays, and the public on Saturdays. Sundays and Mondays would provide the necessary time off for crews to sleep late, relax on the beach, catch up on paperwork, or visit with family.

Working at Windover—though smelly, filthy, and labor-intensive—had its perks. The site's proximity to the coast provided beautiful vistas as summer storms washed across the peninsula, chased by brilliant rainbows that stretched to the horizon. Osprey perched high above the workers' heads, monitoring the progress of the site with their keen eyes. The end of summer brought the best of Florida weather: skies of intense blue streaked with thin cirrus clouds that spread featherlike from west to east; deep shadows that formed late in the day, stretching like dark fingers across the land as the sun shifted to the south; and the clarity of the air as the humidity receded offshore and the winds freshened. One couldn't help but wonder whether the people from Windover, so long ago, had anticipated the shift in season. They must have. The cooler weather would have meant less heat, fewer rains, and far fewer mosquitos. What was the environment in Florida like for people seven thousand years ago? The pond was providing the answers.

SECTION THREE

ANCIENT ENVIRONMENTS

When I was young, I was a serious dinosaur freak. I was obsessed. My mother would buy me books and I'd sit for hours, staring at the artist's renderings of ancient landscapes, which were always depicted in the same way. There were always a variety of species, all grazing happily together in perfect harmony among the swampy grasslands where they lumbered. In the distance a small volcano belched its contents into the sky.

My fascination with dinosaurs grew in concert with my fascination with bones. They were one and the same for many years. The bones of those giant beasts were so beautifully constructed, so perfectly adapted for their environments. I learned to appreciate the human form by studying our ancient predecessors. How disappointing it was to learn that Florida had missed the boat when it came to those amazing giants, for Florida only recently emerged (about 23 million years ago) from the shallow seas that washed over its limestone face and its most ancient surfaces are long buried.

To put Florida's Archaic environment in perspective, we must understand the environmental fluctuations leading up to that period. The last glacial maximum had peaked around eighteen thousand years ago and ecosystems throughout continental North America were still adjusting. The vast Laurentide ice sheet that covered the majority of Canada, reaching all the way down into the upper Midwest, was retreating as global temperatures increased and the massive ice sheets melted. Meltwater streamed into the oceans, raising sea levels by up to one hundred meters in some areas.

In Florida, this period was marked by the inundation of shorelines and the subsequent shrinking of the peninsula by over half. By the time the people of Windover were burying their dead in the pond, the climate had stabilized to near present-day conditions, surface water was approaching what we see today (although the Everglades and Lake

Okeechobee would not form for another couple of thousand years), and the area around the pond was dryer and dominated by oak woodlands.

Radiocarbon dates obtained from the peat provide a depositional chronology for the pond itself. The deepest and therefore earliest layer of peat within the pond is underlain by sand and dated to over 10,000 years ago. Above that, a "rubber peat," characterized by its rubbery consistency, began forming around 8,700 years ago and continued for about 1,000 years. Higher up, the red-brown peat containing the burials dated to around 7,000 years ago. The upper most peat layer that covered the modern base of the pond was deposited around 4,700 years ago.

From the start, Doran and Dickel knew the preservation conditions at Windover would afford a glimpse of the past that far exceeded the people buried within the pond. They would also have the opportunity to learn more about Florida's environment seven thousand years ago. Botanical sampling from the pond began as soon as excavations commenced. By the third season, the results were pouring in.

Samples were taken from materials directly associated with the burials, such as the peat surrounding the bones and that found on some of the brains. Cores—long clear tubes driven deep into the muck—were extracted, sliced open, and sampled. Samples from the tubes were flushed through small sieves to collect delicate plant remains. Botanical samples were corroborated with radiocarbon dates obtained from the cores: one team of researchers would provide the dates of various layers within the cores, while the team of paleobotanists, who specialize in ancient plant use and environments, would identify the plant remains within the dated layers. The dates provided chronological control for the sampling of the plant remains. This corroboration would allow the researchers to know just how long the different plant assemblages had existed in the region and how they changed over time. The plants were identified based on the seeds (macrobotanicals) and pollen they left behind. Once the plants were identified and dated, the environment of seven thousand years ago began to take shape.

Lee Newsom, a graduate student at the University of Florida during the three-year excavation period, analyzed the plant remains from the pond, identifying thirty-one different types of plants found in close association with the burials, nineteen of which have known medicinal applications. These plants included seeds of edible, fleshy fruits such as hackberry, persimmon, red mulberry, prickly pear and wild plum; various types of nuts, such as chestnuts and two types of hickory; and an assortment of vines, herbs, trees, and shrubs.

Many of the plants found in the area today were available to the people of Windover. Cabbage palms grew in abundance, waterlily flanked area ponds, saw palmetto spread in blankets, and hickory trees dropped their dark nuts. Wild grapes, plums, and hackberries hung from nearby bushes and trees; tubers from nutsedge and bulrush were tucked beneath the earth; and knotweed, water hemp, and switch cane produced edible seeds.

These and many other plants were identified by the trace evidence left behind in the peat. The plants not only hinted at what the people from Windover ate, but also indicated the environment in which they lived.

The most intriguing botanical remain was a bottle gourd found buried alongside the body of a young teenager. Identified as *Lagenaria siceraria*, the gourd was radiocarbon dated at around seven thousand years, making it the earliest evidence for bottle gourds north of Mexico. The child was buried face down; the gourd found on the child's back, near the left shoulder. Next to the gourd was a wooden bowl made from live oak and the body was covered in a network of wooden stakes, like many of the burials.

Through the identification and dating of wooden sticks found in direct association with many of the bodies, along with seed and plant remains from the peat, the seasonality of the site was established, indicating the pond was in use during the late summer and early fall months. As the natives moved through the area during the autumn months, whoever died during that period would have been placed in the pond for burial. Where they were living during other times of the year and where they were interring their dead during that time is unknown, but dating of material throughout the pond indicate they utilized the pond as a cemetery for up to 1,000 years, returning generation after generation between 9,000 and 7,900 years ago. The dates within the pond were surprisingly random; the interments did not appear to be sequential in any way and burials spanning the entire period of interment were found throughout the pond.

Newsom surmised that the possible explanation for the seasonal use of the pond was that water levels within the pond were higher in the late summer, early fall months following the summer rainy season. With the pond full, it may have made for a more desirable spot for interment. During the dryer months, when water levels had dropped, perhaps the pond was considered too mucky to attempt interments. One thing the cores confirmed was that the pond had remained wet throughout the last seven thousand years, in spite of seasonal fluctuations.

BEAUTIFUL BURIALS

The third field season opened with relative ease compared to the first two. The wellpoints had been left in place, so setup was reduced to delivering the pumps, establishing the vast network of hoses that would connect the pumps to the wellpoints, and draining the pond.

The second season had produced similar results to the first: few discrete burials encountered with the majority of individuals represented by incomplete or commingled skeletons. Doran and Dickel decided to target two areas of the pond during the third season. They would simultaneously excavate a narrow area in the southwest corner of the pond as well as a larger area to the north. The southwest corner would produce about fifteen burials; the northern section would far exceed their expectations.

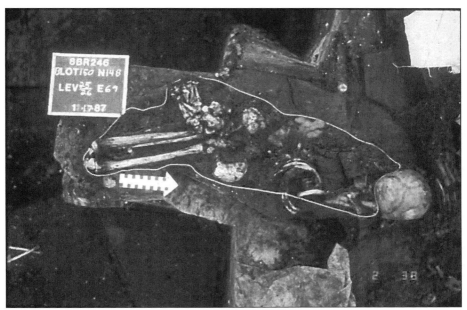

One of the few burials interred face-down. The majority were placed on their left sides in a flexed position. Photo courtesy of R. Brunck.

As the teams started opening the northern section of the pond, suddenly the jumbled remains of the past seasons were replaced by discrete, undisturbed burials, the majority of which were tucked in a "flexed" position on their left sides, their heads generally oriented to the west. Most of the individuals were complete, their bodies in the same positions in which they were buried seven thousand years ago. The process of excavation, transport, reconstruction, conservation, and storage increased to a frenzied pace.

The graves began to speak; each burial hinted at the life of the individual interred. Tucked next to the bodies were beautifully crafted artifacts of bone, wood, antler, and shell, items the individual may have used in life. These items would help recreate life during Florida's Archaic Period.

ANCIENT TOOLS OF THE TRADE

When it came to analyzing the beautiful artifacts from the pond, the task fell to one of Doran's students, Tom Penders. His participation in the Windover excavations set the stage for his career as an archaeologist. Since 2006, Tom has served as the cultural resource manager for the 45th Space Wing at Cape Canaveral Air Station, where he is responsible for cultural resources on Cape property, along with those at Patrick Air Force Base, Malabar Tracking Annex, and Jonathan Dickinson Missile Tracking Annex. He also oversees the cultural resources on the air station's downrange assets on the islands of Ascension and Antigua. Tom's office is part of the Civil Engineering Squadron tucked within their environmental wing, which also houses the folks who oversee programs protecting sea turtle nesting sites and the endangered scrub jay, as well as programs for conducting controlled burns on their lands.

He grew up in southern New Jersey and, like many archaeologists (including yours truly), started out as a dinosaur freak. It wasn't until the age of eight, when he stumbled upon the book *The Splendors of Ancient Egypt,* that he decided then and there he was going to be an archaeologist. His family moved to Titusville when he was in high school, after his father retired from the Atlantic City Electric Company. Late one night, while attending a career night held at his soon-to-be alma mater, Astronaut High School, he talked to a representative from Florida State University, who assured him they had just the program for him. He would later enter FSU's Department of Anthropology in 1980, studying under a young up-and-coming professor, Dr. Glen Doran. Two years later, Doran would take his first trip to check out the mucky pond that would serve as the foundation for both of their careers.

Tom had the good fortune of location and timing. Being at FSU and taking classes under Doran would put Tom smack in the middle of the action once the excavations were underway. Working on his BA and training as an archaeologist set him up as one of about fifteen students who were hired at $4.50 an hour to work on the site. Tom would spend each autumn from 1984 through 1986 excavating at Windover.

When he began working at Windover, he didn't know he would eventually serve as the primary resource for the analysis of the beautifully crafted artifacts streaming from the site. Back then, he didn't care what he was doing, as long as he was digging. After completing his BA in 1985, he stuck around for the final field season, by this time making a whopping $6.50 an hour. He was one of only a handful of individuals that worked all three seasons on the site.

After Windover's final season, Tom went to work as a "dig bum," much like Dickel had done between his degrees. His work took him around the country and beyond. One gig landed him on the shores of Maui, where he worked on the Honokahua Archaeological Project, a cemetery that would eventually produce over three thousand burials. The burials spanned the time when humans first arrived on the islands almost two thousand years ago, up until Captain James Cook arrived in the late 1700s. He spent three months on the island, working in the cemetery and living on the beach.

By 1989, he was ready to continue his education. He attended Northern Arizona University where he studied under Charles Hoffman, who had analyzed artifacts from Silver Springs, Florida. Tom began studying artifacts as well, having already spent several years captivated by Native American production of stone points. He was planning to analyze the artifacts from Windover as the subject of his master's thesis when health complications drew him back to Florida. He contacted Doran, who offered him a spot in FSU's grad program, and before he knew it, Tom was right back on track, completing his graduate courses and spending hours poring over the artifacts from Windover.

Tom's fascination with artifacts was multifocal. He was not only interested the types of materials the people from Windover had chosen for their tools, he was also interested in the techniques involved in their production and their application in daily life. He decided to examine them based on these areas of interest. Here is what he discovered.

Artifacts made from bone, stone, antler, and faunal teeth were recovered from Burial 90, which contained an 11-year-old and a neonate. Photo courtesy of R. Brunck.

First, there were the materials. Bone played a prominent role in the production of tools, weapons, and utilitarian objects, but the people from Windover were utilizing a plethora of materials to construct the objects needed to carve out an existence in the wilds of Florida. Wood and antler objects were present in abundance. Tom was captivated by their variation and exceptional craftsmanship.

A total of 119 artifacts made from various parts of animals were recovered from the pond. Tom divided the items up in twenty-seven functional categories for the purpose of analysis, based on their function. The artifacts were recovered from thirty-three burials, yet many of the items were found among commingled remains or were not associated with a particular burial. Hunting and fishing implements were made from deer antler and bone, and manatee rib. These materials

91

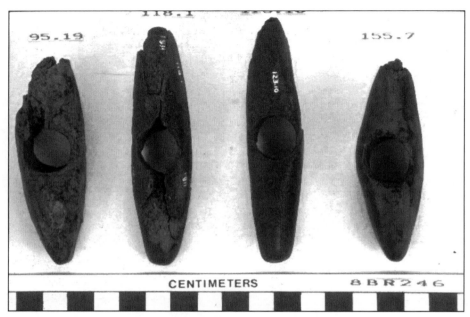

These artifacts are believed to be atlatl handles and antler shaft straighteners. Photo courtesy of R. Brunck.

were fashioned into cups and weights that went on the ends of atlatls, which were used to propel spears. An atlatl is a narrow, flattened, wooden implement that has a grooved handle at one end, a small hook or cup at the other. The tool is typically between one and two meters long and has a groove down its center, where a spear is placed and butted up against the hook or cup at its end. It is thrown as if throwing a baseball—overhand in a large arc. The atlatl extends the length of the throwing arm, which increases the thrower's range of motion, and the weight attached on the underside of its hook end provides thrust. A skilled atlatl hunter could hit a target up to one hundred yards away. Atlatls were used in Florida in place of the bow and arrow, which was never invented or adopted by aboriginals in the area.

Other hunting items included projectile points and barbed fishing hooks, both made from antler. These were probably attached to long wooden handles and used to hunt small animals, such as raccoon or rabbits, or for killing birds and fish, perhaps as the group moved

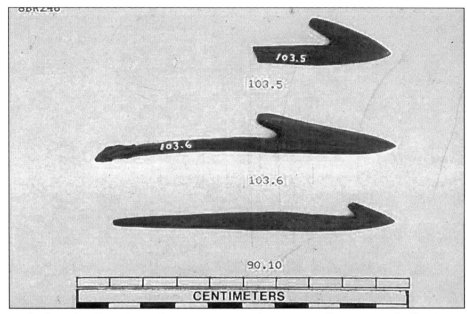

Barbed projectile points: the center point shows a small amount of adhesive still adhering to its base. Photo courtesy of R. Brunck.

between camp sites, what Tom refers to as "hunting on the fly." The atlatls, with their weighted ends, could also be used in a pinch to club small prey.

There was a very small number of stone points recovered from the pond. Only seven lithics were found, six of them made from chert, one from limestone. According to Dr. Samuel Upchurch from the University of Central Florida, the chert material came from the Panasoffkee cluster found in Sumter County, located just west of Leesburg, in the central part of the state. One of the points was part of a large tool cache buried alongside a young girl around the age of ten. The single limestone point was not associated with a burial, but recovered from the wall of an excavation unit mixed in with sand that had been brought in from west Florida as packing around one of the wellpoints. Its association with the burials at Windover, therefore, is questionable.

Some of the tools at Windover were actually used in the production of other tools. Pressure flakers were made from antler, gravers (used

These are the only projectile points recovered from the pond. The stone originated from the Panasofkee quarry cluster, located over 80 miles from the
pond. Photo courtesy of R. Brunck.

for incising objects), and scrapers from shark's teeth; shaft straighteners used to straighten arrows or spears were made from bone, wood,
and antler; and gravers and burnishers (used for flattening or polish-
ing) were made from the teeth of opossums and canids (possibly dog).

There were tools used for butchering, made from the limb bones of
deer. These same bones were used to create awls—sharp tools that can
be used for punching holes through leather. Perforators and punches
made from antler would have also been used to work hides.

These tools would have provided the people of Windover the objects
necessary for hunting, butchering, and the processing of meat; the collecting and preparation of plants; and the production of clothing made
from hides and possibly plants (moss, palms, and grasses).

The artifact assemblage also included ornamental objects that may
have been worn in life or used as ceremonial objects. Four carved
tubes, each about ten centimeters in length, were made from bird
bone, perhaps pelican or heron. Three of the tubes were decorated with

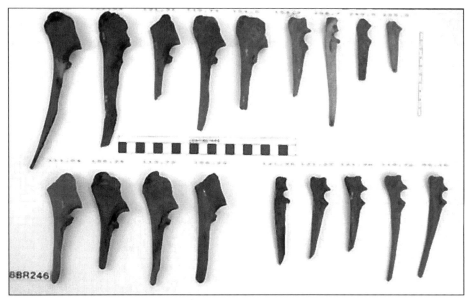

Faunal bone was used extensively to create awls, or punching tools. Photo courtesy of R. Brunck.

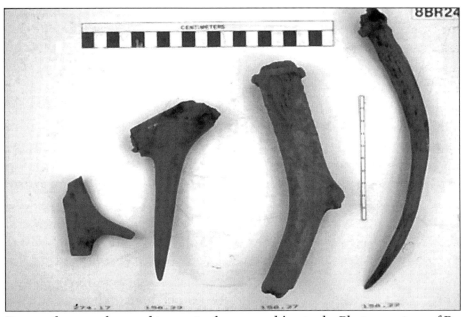

Deer antler was also used to create sharp punching tools. Photo courtesy of R. Brunck.

95

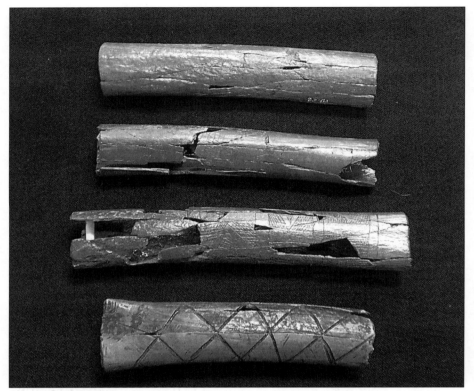

Four bird-bone tubes were recovered, some intricately incised. Photo by Wentz.

inscribed geometric lines; one of these has elaborate hachure decorations. The incisions were made with a sharp object, perhaps a shark's tooth engraver. Other decorative items were made from bone, shell, seeds, and beads. A necklace made from the vertebrae of a fish, probably catfish, was found in position across the neck area of a young female in her early twenties. Also around her neck were two other necklaces, one made from the seeds of a Sabal palm, the other from ground shells. Another necklace made from forty-three shell beads and thirteen Sabal palm seeds was found around the neck of a two-year-old. No string or cordage was found with these necklaces.

Containers made from turtle shell were also found which may have been used in the preparation of medicinal plants. Four containers were

One of four turtle shell containers found alongside burials. Photo by Wentz.

recovered, three of them buried with females, one with a child. The containers were made by separating the carapace or top of the shell from its bottom, the plastron. Separation was accomplished by sawing the articulations until the two sections could be pulled apart.

The final category of items may have had a very special function. Nine hollow-point awls, made from either bobcat or canid species; needles made from canid leg bones; and pins made from deer bone may have been used in the production of materials that represented one of the most astounding finds at Windover: handwoven textiles.

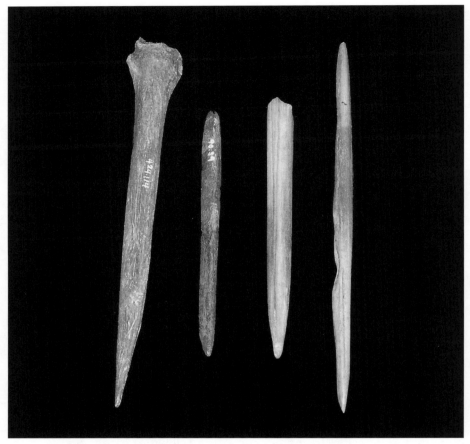

Pins and awls made from bone and antler were polished and sharpened. Photo by Wentz.

WRAPPING THE DEAD

At the end of the second season, as the last few burials were carefully lifted from the ground, Dickel noted faint remnants of an unknown material adhering to some of the bones. They teased tiny fragments of the material from the bones and peat where they had degraded to the point of disintegration when handled. It wasn't until the third season and the recovery of the discrete, undisturbed burials that Doran and Dickel finally got a good look at the strange substance found next to some of the bones and were astonished to find it was cloth.

When the excavations began, Doran and Dickel knew the site had potential for the recovery of objects and materials that are usually lost over time due to the unforgiving nature of the archaeological record, especially in Florida. But the conditions at Windover were unique, the preservation exceptional. The recovery of brain matter had already proven that the pond had the potential for producing some of the most exciting materials yet recovered in North America. The new material they were finding simply added to the site's extraordinary inventory.

The material first showed up as faint traces against bone. At first, the excavators weren't sure what they were seeing: if it was simply a thin layer of peat that had adhered to the bone or if it was something more, something separate from the earth matrix. It wasn't until a larger fragment was found that they realized that the material had texture and a pattern to it. They were definitely dealing with textiles.

The textiles were a nightmare to excavate. They were thin, degraded, and easy to confuse with the peat, since in some cases they had degraded to such an extent that they appeared continuous with the muck. Although identifying them was difficult, the real challenge came when they had to remove them from the pond. This required ingenuity on the part of the excavators. First, they would photograph, map, and draw the fabrics in place before removal was attempted. Once the materials were documented, they were loosened from the bone (when

A piece of intricately woven textile, photographed after it has been treated with a consolidant. Photo courtesy of R. Brunck.

possible) using small instruments and painstaking technique. The larger pieces were even more problematic. Since they couldn't be lifted from the burials, they decided the safest means of excavation were to remove the entire burial in a single block, fabric and all.

They framed out boxes, which were placed around the pedestalled burial containing the textiles and the entire burial was then undercut using sharp tools. A base was fixed to the box, handles were secured to its outer perimeter, and the burial was removed in its entirety. Once the burial was secured in the box, it was carried from the pond. Removal required many hands; the blocks of earth were extremely heavy, their cargo extremely fragile. They worked in teams to walk the boxes out of the pond, carefully using wooden planks as stepping stones so as not to crush the surrounding burials.

The textiles needed special care. They would require considerable conservation and a specialist experienced in the preservation and anal-

Excavators haul away a burial wrapped in textile. The entire block of earth was removed as a unit. Photo courtesy of R. Brunck.

ysis of ancient textiles. So Doran contacted one of the top researchers in the field, James Adovasio.

The materials were originally sent to the Perishables Analysis Facility at the University of Pittsburgh for treatment and analysis. The research facility itself was later transferred to the R. L. Andrews Center for Perishables Analysis at Mercyhurst College and the Windover textiles went with it.

The Andrews Center is an impressive research lab. Originally known as the Basket Lab, the facility specializes in the analysis of ancient perishables, including cordage, clothing, basketry, bags, and sandals from archaeological sites from around the world. Some of the most renowned sites in their inventory include textile impressions from Dolni Vestonice, a thirty-thousand-year-old burial site located near the modern town of Brno in eastern Czech Republic; basketry from Meadowcroft Rockshelter located in Pennsylvania, and considered the most ancient human habitation site in North America; and cordage from the famed Monte Verde site in Chile, dating over thirteen thousand years ago. Dr. Adovasio directs research at the center. He was just the person needed for the delicate textiles from Windover.

Eighty-seven perishable fiber artifacts were recovered from the pond. They represented sixty-seven original items recovered from the burials, many of which had been torn into fragments as they disintegrated over time. Conservation began in the field. When textiles were identified, they were kept moist by continuously misting their surfaces, using small spray bottles of water. When they were removed from the ground, they were also kept moist and placed in plastic bags or, for the larger sections removed in boxes, covered with plastic sheeting. The plastic bags were placed in Styrofoam coolers. They were stored in a temporary on-site field laboratory and were treated with PEG: the same polyethylene glycol that had been originally used on the bones. The materials were then shipped via Federal Express to the lab in Pittsburgh. The two large boxed blocks, Burials 73 and 82, were flown as passengers aboard a U.S. Air flight to their new home.

Once they arrived at the lab, they were placed in a special climate-controlled chamber that maintained a cool forty-five degrees at 80-90 percent humidity, but after some experimentation, the temperature and humidity were adjusted down to around thirty-five degrees at 55 percent. These conditions prevented the fabrics from drying out and also prevented mold from growing on their surfaces. On the occasion when mold did crop up, they were spot-treated with a combination liquid of isopropyl alcohol, ethanol, and deionized water. If the mold grew on the container itself, it was treated with a good dose of Lysol.

Treatment of the fabrics began by immersing them in deionized water in order to remove the mineral salts with which they had become impregnated during their long stint in the pond. But, as the salts were removed, the bacteria moved in. Lab personnel initially tried treating the materials with ampicillin. When this failed, they tried several other treatments with little success. Numerous outside specialists were consulted about the bacteria and fungus growing on the specimens. Suggestions for treatment included a dunking in bleach, a quick formaldehyde bath, a bombardment with gamma rays, and if all else failed, Borax. All of these suggestions were rejected; the materials were

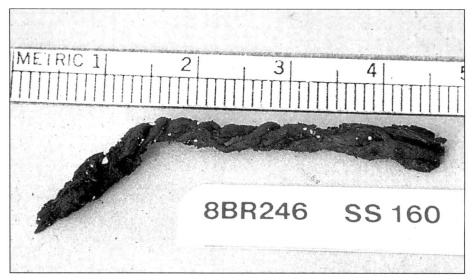

A piece of the intricate twining recovered from one of the burials. Photo courtesy of R. Brunck.

simply too precious to risk using such aggressive treatments. They finally decided the safest and most thorough means of ridding the materials of the unwanted pests was via soaking the fabrics in either 40 percent isopropyl or 70 percent ethanol solution. The treatment was a success and this regimen has been used as the lab's antimicrobial treatment of choice ever since.

Once the desalinization was complete, the samples would be conserved and then freeze-dried. The materials were immersed in a PEG bath and they were then flash-frozen and stored in a deep freezer at (minus) -20 degrees Fahrenheit. Once frozen, the materials were then treated with a cutting-edge conservation treatment known as Parylene. Parylene is a polymer which provides stabilization of fragile materials. First discovered in 1947, it was introduced to the field of conservation in the 1980s as a means of conserving archival and artifactual materials. One of its first success stories was the application and conservation of a piece of 45-million-year-old forest debris recovered from a site in the arctic. When applied to the Windover materials, the bits of fabric were strengthened and preserved, allowing their analysis to begin.

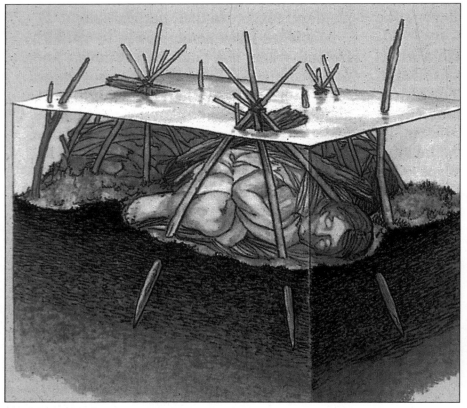

An artist's rendering shows a cutaway of the pond containing burials. Photo courtesy of G. Doran.

Although all the materials were handmade, their design and means of manufacture varied. The materials represented a range of items produced and used by the people from Windover. These included basketry, textiles, and cordage. The textiles were further divided into types: there were forty-nine pieces of twining and one example of a plain weave. The cordage was produced in two forms: they were either spun and twisted or braided.

The materials were made from palm fibers, most likely cabbage palm or possibly saw palmetto. The palms were possibly scraped with a rigid tool, perhaps a flaked stone tool, a wooden scraper, or a sharpened piece of shell, or by using one's teeth.

All of the materials were found directly associated with human remains and approximately half of all burials at Windover contained these materials in some form. The individuals were typically placed in a flexed position and wrapped in the textiles, along with items they may have used in life, such as tools and ornaments. The entire bundle was then carried out into the water and submerged beneath the surface. The body was pushed down into the base of the pond and anchored in place using wooden stakes. Many of the wooden stakes were driven through the margins of the textiles and down into the surrounding soils. These stakes served to anchor the body to the base of the pond and protect it from predators. Apparently the stakes were effective. Out of the more than ten thousand individual bones recovered from the pond, only six contained any sign of carnivore damage. Remnants of grass bundles were also found with the fabrics. These may have served as linings within the bundles.

Some of the materials were encrusted with a yellowish-red coating, which turned out to be remnants of deer hide that may have also covered the burials. Some of the materials contained pollen that had become lodged within their fibers, most likely from pine trees nearby.

One of the tapered wooden sticks used to cover the burials and anchor them to the base of the pond. Photo courtesy of G. Doran.

The presence of such pollen may indicate that the materials were made during the spring, when pollen from pine trees is most abundant.

The fabrics from Windover represent the oldest example of these styles of handwoven textiles in the New World. Older samples of perishables—handmade items fashioned from animal or plant fibers—have been found in North, Central, and South America, although the number of sites producing perishable items in North America, some of which date to over eleven thousand years, is less than ten. The Windover fabrics are the oldest perishable materials yet discovered in Florida, although it is safe to say that the production and use of basketry in the region predates the Windover site, as it does in other areas around the country. At sites such as Little Salt Spring, materials originally misidentified as tapa or bark cloth were recovered and possibly date to around five thousand years ago.

That these materials played an important role in the mortuary practices at Windover is without doubt. The percentage of people buried in fabric and the number of beautifully constructed items placed alongside the bodies speaks to the complex rituals surrounding the use of the pond as a cemetery. The fabrics from Windover remind us of the skill and craftsmanship of people in Florida over seven thousand years ago and the care with which they treated their dead.

THE BONES SPEAK

We finally turn to the bones themselves. The examination of human skeletal remains from archaeological sites provides a glimpse into the health of historic and prehistoric populations. Through their analysis, we can gauge how well nourished they were, how they adapted to their environment, and explore illness and injury among ancient peoples.

But the analysis of skeletal remains was not always considered an integral part of archaeological studies. Prior to the 1980s, data on human remains consisted primarily of the age and sex of the individual at death and was usually relocated to the appendices of reports. Most early studies of human remains focused on description of pathological processes at the individual level, one skeleton at a time, which provided limited information on issues concerning past health.

For example, say we find a single skeleton in a burial. We can identify the sex of the individual and the age at death and even investigate any signs of illness or injury they may have experienced during life, but it tells us only a single story. In contrast, when we have a population the size of Windover, we can observe trends, which provide a better overall glimpse of what life was actually like for those living long ago. We can obtain the average life span by comparing ages at death; we can observe the prevalence of traumatic injuries and infer levels of violence and interpersonal conflict; and we can examine their teeth and count the average number of cavities each person sustained and how many teeth were typically lost prior to death within the population. We can explore a range of health issues that leave their evidence on the bones, but only by making comparisons can we elucidate the broader issues of health in the past. How do we do this? Through bioarchaeology.

The term "bioarchaeology" was first coined by Jane Buikstra, one of the founders of this subfield of biological anthropology. The term was intended to describe the new multidisciplinary approach required for the analysis of human remains. Archaeologists no longer merely

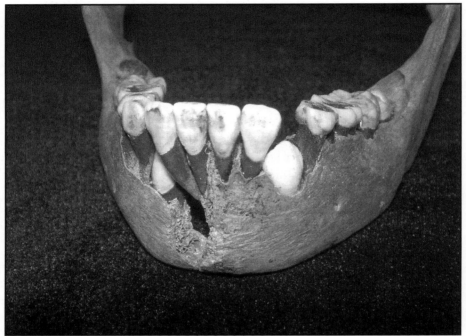

The mixed dentition of a child, showing permanent canines erupting. Photo by Wentz.

counted the number of individuals in a cemetery assemblage; now they wanted detailed information as to who the individuals were during life and what their physical life experiences entailed. Bioarchaeology provided the perfect set of analytical tools for the job. Bioarchaeology allows us to address issues of nutrition, disease, physiological stress, activity-related skeletal changes, and quality of life in past populations.

The analysis begins by determining the age, sex, and height of each individual in the assemblage. Age is obtained based on changes on the surfaces of certain bones, primarily the pelvis, that occur as the individual ages. These surfaces become more rough and porous over time and provide an age estimate, which tells us how old someone was at the time they died. We can also use the rate of suture closures on the skull and palate, which fuse together over time as the individual ages, although these are less reliable than the surfaces of the pelvis. Determining the age of a child at death can be accomplished by examining the eruption of their teeth. Since we know, on average, when the decid-uous (milk) and permanent teeth erupt in children, we can determine how old they were at the time of death based on which teeth have come in and which have been lost.

Sex is assessed based on the size and shape of the skeleton. The skull and pelvis are the best elements to use, since the majority of the physi-cal features associated with our sex are expressed in these areas. The skulls of males tend to be more robust, with greater muscle attachment sites. The pelvis of a male is shaped very differently from a female, mainly because it is not designed to accommodate the passage of the fetus during delivery, as is the female's.

Assessing sex in children is a bit more complex, since the skeleton doesn't exhibit the characteristic changes associated with sex until after puberty. Therefore, unless sex can be identified through DNA analysis (Y chromosomes for males, X for females), children are labeled "ambiguous."

Height is based on the length of long bones. The femur is the bone of choice. It is the largest, strongest bone in the body and tends to pre-

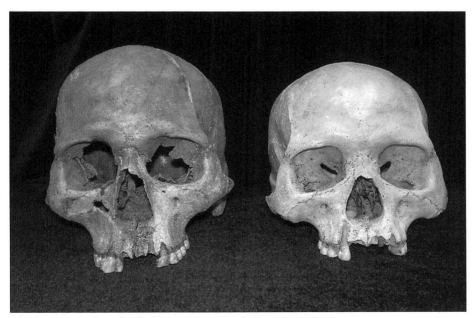

Well-preserved male (left) and female skulls. Photo by Wentz.

serve better than smaller, more fragile bones of the skeleton. By measuring the length of the femur and working the measurement through a regression formula, we can determine the height of the individual based on the bone's length. Other bones can be used, but the femur is the most common.

Once we have the age, sex, and height of each individual, we can begin to make comparisons within the populations. How many are male? How many are female? What was the average life span among the individuals represented? What was the mortality rate for the children? How tall was the average individual? All of these questions can be answered once the preliminary data is collected.

We can also assess population origins and their movements over time. Today, this is best accomplished via DNA analysis, but the skeleton itself can aid in this quest. By taking specific measurements, primarily of the skull, we can input those measurements into statistical databases which match the measurements to populations that have been assessed throughout the world. People who live close to each other tend to breed. That breeding results in the sharing of physical traits, such as body form, head size, skin color, and hair texture. That is why Asians look Asian, Caucasians look Caucasian, and Africans look African; individuals carry the traits of their ancestors wherever they go and spread them as they multiply. Thus, if we examine the physical traits of past populations, we are able to match them with the populations from which they originated.

The last major category of information we collect from the skeleton is based on health. There are a whole set of pathological processes that show up on the skeleton. Then again, there are many that don't. An individual can die from a sudden illness, such as the flu, without it ever impacting the skeleton. That is why in many cases, the exact cause of death cannot be determined in many archaeological skeletons.

However, many disease processes do show up on the skeleton, and we'll discuss how they show up in a moment. First, why do we care about pathology among ancient skeletons? We care because health is directly related to lifestyle. The more we know about past health, the more we can say about how their health was impacted by the way they made their living. Whether a person was a hunter-gatherer or an agriculturalist, a nomad or sedentary, whether they ate a variety of foods or relied on more restricted food stuffs will determine what type of health they experienced during life. So what do we know about the people of Windover?

As the skeletons came out of the ground, Doran and Dickel collected information as to the age of each individual at Windover. Below is a graph showing the age at death of the population. As you can see, child mortality was high, with the largest number of child deaths taking place prior to the age of ten. This high mortality would explain why over half the burials within the pond were those of children. You can also see that age at death peaked in the late forties, which appears to be the average lifespan at Windover, although there were some individuals who lasted well into their sixties, attesting to the hearty nature of these people.

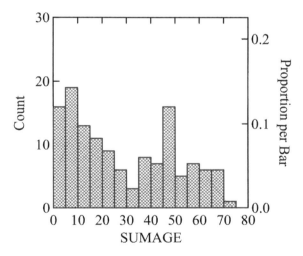

As for the sex distribution within the cemetery, among the adults it was about an equal ration of males to females. Since the sex of the children is indeterminate, we don't know their ratios.

The average height of the females was around five feet tall; that of males, around five-and-a-half feet. Height is a central theme in data collection among human remains. In forensic contexts, it helps investigators match the remains to missing persons. In bioarchaeological studies, the height an individual attained in life is used to assess levels of nutrition, since individuals who are well-nourished tend to grow taller. Yes, height is genetically determined to an extent, as well. If you have short parents, more than likely, you'll also be short, although there are always exceptions to the rule. This is where population studies come into play. By assessing the average height of a population, bioarchaeologists can assess levels of health among the population by correlating height with levels of nutrition and incidence of pathology. Populations who eat nutritious foods and suffer from low incidences of disease tend to be taller than poorly nourished populations with high rates of pathology.

Once the basic demographics of the cemetery were established, the foundation was laid for future studies of their overall health. Although it came over twenty years after the site's discovery, my research of the Windover skeletons would afford a glimpse into issues of health among these ancient people. We will now examine life and death among the people at Windover.

HEALTH AT WINDOVER

The types and levels of pathology among ancient populations provide great insight into what life was like for people living in the past. For me, looking at a human skeleton that lived thousands of years ago and yet suffered from some of the same illnesses or injuries we encounter today is one of the most impactful moments in archaeology. To look upon an individual with severe dental disease or someone in the advanced stages of arthritis and try to picture what their life was like on a daily basis can certainly make you appreciate the marvels of modern medicine at our disposal today.

Such was the case with Windover. The hours I spent poring over their remains was a lesson in humility. To see the extent of some of the pathological processes that had inundated their bones reminded me of the degree of human suffering endured by ancient peoples.

Their illnesses as well as their injuries came in many forms. We'll discuss some of these now. I have broken the types of pathology into general categories to simplify the overview. Keep in mind that although the types of pathologies and conditions are extensive, what we see on the bones themselves is only a partial representation of what the individual suffered from in life. Many of the skeletons from Windover show no obvious cause of death. Why they ended up in the pond remains a mystery.

INFECTION

Many people think of bone as a solid, unchanging substance within the body, but in reality it is a dynamic tissue that responds to disease and injury just like any other bodily tissue. Infection is one of the forms of pathology that can severely affect bone. It typically shows up as a thickening of the outer layer of the bone, resulting in inflammation of its surface, known as *periostitis*. It is usually the result of an infection, but can also occur secondary to a traumatic injury, for example if someone suffers a broken bone where the bone ends protrude through the skin. The break in the skin's surface allows bacteria to enter the area and can result in infection of the bone itself. The infection can spread to other bones or infect the bone's inner cavity, known as the marrow space, resulting in a serious condition called *osteomyelitis*. The usual culprits of osteomyelitis are *Staphylococcus* and *Streptococcus* microorganisms. These pus producers cause enlargement of the

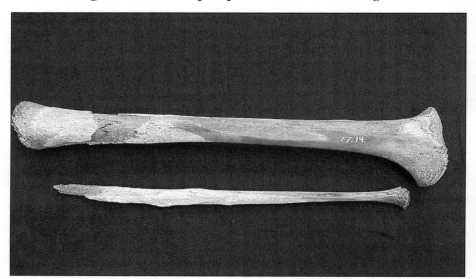

Lower leg bones (tibia and fibula) of a child showing signs of infection (*periostitis*), exhibited as the white outer layer on the bones. Photo courtesy of G. Sutton.

114

bone itself, and in extreme cases, can result in an evacuation hole in the bone through which the pus escapes into surrounding tissues, spreading the infection.

Evidence of bone infection may indicate stress within a population in the form of malnutrition, decreased immune resistance, and can result in high rates of death. Bone inflammation can also be caused by infectious diseases, such as tuberculosis and syphilis.

The majority of people at Windover showed no sign of infection. About 10 percent showed signs of infection on their tibia, which is a common area for periostitis to occur, since the surface of the tibia that makes up our shin area is typically thin, with little protective tissue to ward off infections that occur on the outside of the leg. The thin tissue also provides little protection against traumatic injury, which can introduce infectious organisms into the bone through cuts or fractures. Systemic infection, which is indicated by infection on multiple bones in the body, only affected a small number of people at Windover.

TRAUMA

Trauma is another common condition in the archaeological record. Traumatic injury, in contrast to some infectious processes such as influenza, is more likely to involve bone, thus is easier to track among ancient populations. If you hit someone with a blunt object, chances are you'll strike bone. That's why trauma analysis makes up the majority of pathologies tracked among ancient human remains.

Trauma is a physical injury or wound caused by external force and can affect the skeleton in a number of ways. It can result in a break in the bone (fracture), a dislocation of a joint, or a deformity. Traumatic injuries within ancient populations provide a great deal of information about people's daily activities and the physical challenges they encountered. Such was the case at Windover. Arm, leg, skull, hand, and facial fractures were present, although the majority of the fractures appear to be accidental in nature. There was little evidence of interpersonal vio-

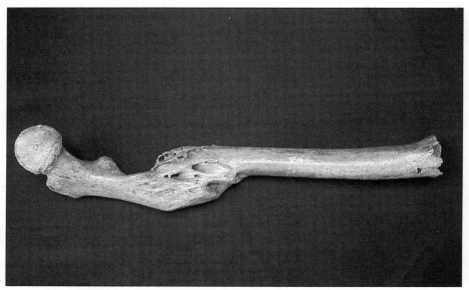

The fractured femur of a woman who was able to heal from the injury, yet must have walked with an extreme limp. Photo courtesy of G. Sutton.

lence, such as weapon wounds to the head or high levels of fractures to the face. The majority of the broken bones were to the arms, perhaps from falls while traversing the tangled terrain of Florida.

The one exception was a young male found with an antler tine embedded in his hip. There was no evidence that the bone had started to heal, so the injury probably resulted in the man's death or at least contributed to it. There was another hint to his cause of death: while his skeleton was fairly complete, he was missing his head.

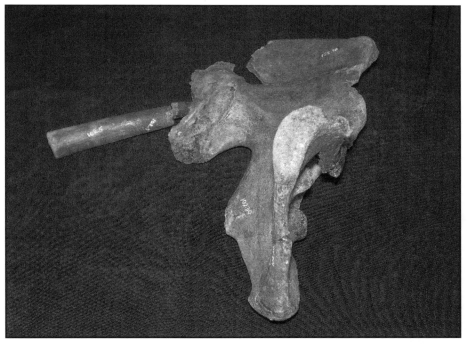

This antler tine is embedded in the hip of a young male. The wound shows no sign of healing and therefore must have happened around the time of death. Photo by Wentz.

Nutrition

Stable isotope analyses and archaeobotanical reconstruction have provided much information as to the types of foods utilized at Windover. Noreen Turross, who at the time was a researcher at the Smithsonian Institution conducted stable isotope analyses from Windover, examing the ratios of carbon and nitrogen isotopes in order to determine the types of foods the Windover people relied on. Her research indicated a "riverine" diet consisting of such items as duck, turtle, and catfish. They would have most likely been supplementing their diet with deer, especially considering the large number of deer bones that were used for the creation of tools. Although the area provided a broad range of nutritional items that were exploited by the Windover population, their bones reveal evidence of periodic shortage. These periods could have been caused by seasonal fluctuations such as drought, which could have impacted the availability of plant and animal food sources.

There are several signs of inadequate nutrition, what we refer to as *biological stress*, that show up on the skeleton. The most common areas on the skeleton that are assessed for signs of nutritional inadequacies are the orbits of the eyes and the top of the head. These areas are prone to develop small clusters of pin-prick-sized holes and are linked to inadequate vitamins in the diet, heavy parasite loads in the gut (which can sap the body of iron), and malnutrition caused by diarrheal diseases.

These porous lesions in the orbits, known as *cribra orbitalia,* were common among the people at Windover. Twenty-nine individuals showed signs of this condition, although it was probably much more frequent. Many of the skeletons are lacking skulls, so a true count of this condition is unknown. Among the children whose skulls were preserved, the condition was even more common. But one thing I noticed when examining the orbits of the children was that even though the

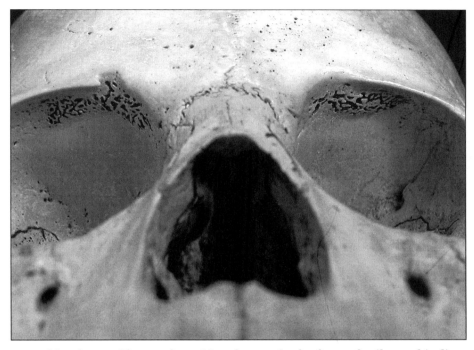

Eye orbits show evidence of nutritional stress in the form of *cribra orbitalia.*
Photo courtesy of G. Sutton.

condition was common among the very young, if the child was fortunate enough to make it into their teens, most of the cases of cribra had healed or were in the process of healing. This indicates the children were most stressed during the years prior to their teens. By the time they reached their teen years, they seemed to be on a path to better nutrition.

Incidences of cribra orbitalia and its associated condition affecting the top of the skull, *porotic hyperostosis,* were higher among the females at Windover. This may be related to the stress of pregnancy, which places an added burden on a woman's nutritional needs since the fetus takes precedence over the mother's needs while in utero.

Nutritional deficiencies can have serious implications for the health of the individual and subsequently the overall health of a population. Lack of certain vitamins, such as vitamin D, can lead to conditions such as rickets, which results in softening of the bones and bowing of the

119

legs. Lack of vitamin C can lead to scurvy, which can result in dental disease and thinning of the bones, since it slows the production of new bone cells.

Enamel Defects

Another sign of biological stress results in the formation of lines, pits, and grooves found on the surfaces of teeth, known as *linear enamel hypoplasias* (LEH). These defects result from an interruption of the development of the enamel layer of the tooth. If someone suffers from serious infection or inadequate nutrition during their early years when the enamel layer is forming, these lines or pits can develop due to interruptions in the laying down of the enamel. You can see these defects on people today. The next time you speak to someone, check out their teeth. If they show striations across their surfaces, you can bet they suffered from some form of biological stress when they were very young.

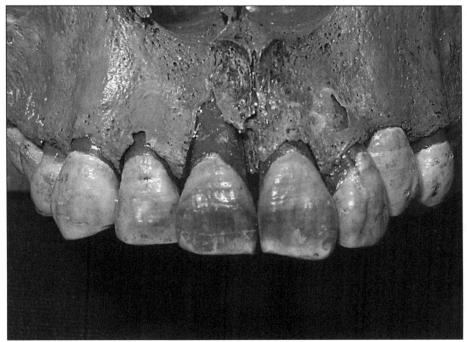

Teeth of a child exhibit growth arrest lines (*linear enamel hypoplasia*). Photo courtesy of G. Sutton.

121

DEGENERATIVE JOINT DISEASE

Degenerative joint disease, what we commonly call arthritis, is a condition that results from mechanical wear and tear on the joints due to repetitive activity. It produces bony deposits known as *osteophytes* around the periphery of joint surfaces, and in severe cases may lead to complete loss of mobility of the joint resulting from bony fusion within the joint. Usually, the more physically demanding the lifestyle, the greater the incidence and severity the degenerative bony changes are. However, average life span can affect rates of degenerative joint disease within skeletal populations since the older the individual, the

Lumbar vertebra shows bony lipping (*osteophytosis*) around the rim of its body. Photo courtesy of G. Sutton.

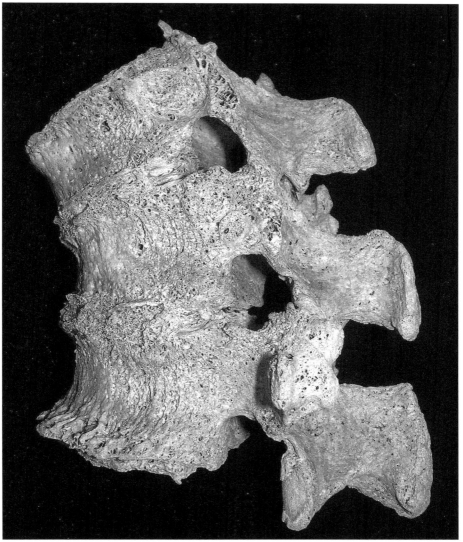

Fused vertebrae of a woman who suffered from extreme *osteophytosis*. Photo courtesy of G. Sutton.

greater likelihood that he or she will display these bony changes over time.

Among Windover, arthritis was a common occurrence. Shoulders, knees, vertebrae and hands showed evidence of their rugged lifestyle. Carrying heavy loads, walking over long distances, and performing the manual tasks of production would, over time, cause wear and tear of the joints, resulting in the characteristic changes related to arthritis. The most common area on the body for arthritis among the Windover people was among the vertebrae. Males tended to have more arthritis of the knees and vertebrae, possibly tied to walking long distances during hunting. The women showed more degeneration of the shoulders and elbows, which might be related to tasks they performed in life, such as the preparation of hides or plant products.

Although degenerative joint disease can be indicative of heavy mechanical load, it is also highly correlated with normal age-related changes. Considering the number of individuals within the Windover population above the age of forty, the elevated number of vertebrae involved could simply be a reflection of normal degenerative changes present among the elderly within a population. This could also be the case with degenerative changes of the shoulder and elbow and the hip and knee.

DENTAL HEALTH

Teeth are often the only part of the body that survives in the archaeological record. They can provide valuable information concerning diet, oral hygiene, stress, occupation, cultural behavior, and subsistence of past peoples. Cavities, abscesses, inflammation of the gums, and tooth loss have been common occurrences throughout man's history. At Windover, we can get an idea of just how rough life was in the Archaic Period by glancing at the people's teeth. Let's imagine for a moment . . .

It's seven thousand years ago and you live in Florida among a small group of hunter-gatherers. You must hunt and collect all your food and

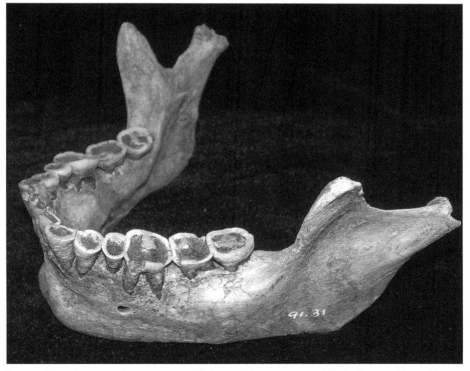

Lower jaw shows extreme wear of the teeth common at Windover. Photo by Wentz.

125

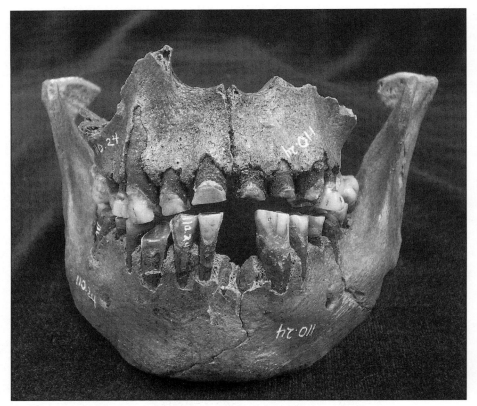

Jaws show wear patterns indicative of using the teeth as tools. Photo by Wentz.

water, build your shelters, make all your clothing, and produce your own tools and utensils. Life is all about work. On top of that, there's no air conditioning, no such thing as bug spray, and—to make matters worse—you have a large abscess that is slowly eating away the lower left side of your jaw.

As I've studied the bones of Windover, I've often been amazed how so many of them could survive with such serious dental disease. These were true pioneers. Cavities weren't their biggest problem. Because they wore their teeth down so quickly and so thoroughly, most cavities were erased over time as the high levels of grit in their diets worked like sand paper on the surfaces of their teeth, reducing them to flattened nubs by the time they reached their forties. They were also using their teeth as tools, which combined with the grit to produce interesting wear patterns throughout their mouths. Some of their front teeth had been worn into high arches. Others appeared to have used their teeth for gripping items in the sides of their mouths, producing grooves along their side teeth.

Dental abscesses, which develop following the infiltration of bacteria into the pulp cavity of the tooth, can be life threatening if untreated. As the bacteria accumulate, pus is produced, which puts pressure on the surrounding bone. The pressure eventually causes a hole to open up in the bone, which allows the release of pus into surrounding tissues. If the bacteria within the pus make it into the bloodstream, it can lead to infection throughout the body and eventual death. Based on the high number of abscesses at Windover, they must have been a constant source of pain and sickness among its inhabitants.

Many teeth were lost prior to death, what bioarchaeologists refer to as *antemortem tooth loss*. Tooth loss is characteristic of poor dental health. If your gums are unhealthy, they become inflamed. This

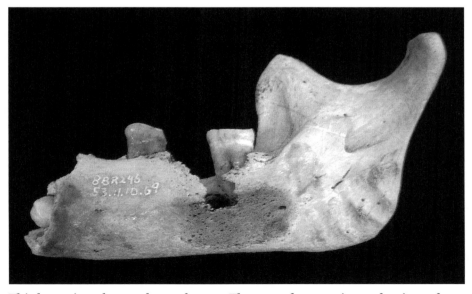

This lower jaw shows a large abscess. The wound was active at the time of death, and therefore may have caused the death of the individual. Photo courtesy of G. Sutton.

inflammation can cause problems within the bones of the jaws, which can eventually result in the loosening of teeth. Once they are loose, they tend to fall out. Tooth loss was higher among the males. The men lost about 10 percent of their teeth prior to death, compared to only around 8 percent for the females.

HEALTH AND THE ENVIRONMENT

Just like today, the health of individuals seven thousand years ago was directly tied to their environment. In developed countries, people can mitigate much of the environmental impact to their health. But for the people of Windover, their environment had a tremendous impact on their health and nutrition, since they were completely dependent on their surroundings for survival. Here we will explore some of the environmental factors that would have contributed to poor health among the people at Windover.

During the period when the people from Windover were utilizing the pond for the interment of their dead, climatic and sea level fluctuations were tapering off. Pollen profiles indicate a dry oak woodland over much of the peninsula. Marshes, wetlands, and cypress swamps dotted the landscape. The subtropical climate combined with numerous water sources would have provided environmental conditions perfectly suited for invertebrates such as leeches, worms, mites, and spiders. They would have coexisted alongside the people of Windover.

Parasites would also have been present. They are spread to humans through ingestion, by contact with soil infected with fecal matter, by consumption of meat containing larvae, and from mosquito bites, and would have had a negative impact on health at Windover. Sites in California have produced fossilized feces, known as *coprolites*, which have revealed the presence of hookworms that would have wreaked havoc on the individual during life. Another source of infectious disease in early hunter-gatherers could have been their ingestion of infected meat from the animals they hunted. A number of infectious organisms can be transmitted via animals, such as anthrax, toxoplasmosis, taeniasis (tape worms), and possibly tuberculosis and influenza.

Hookworm infestation today remains endemic to the tropics and subtropics. The World Health Organization estimates that about 25

129

percent of the world's population is affected. Once the worms reach the small intestine, they anchor and engorge with blood before reaching the adult stage. Heavy worm burdens can produce iron-deficiency anemia secondary to significant blood loss, making infants especially susceptible to hemorrhagic shock.

Climate would have also played a role in the transmission of pathogens among the people of Windover. Warm weather provides suitable environments for the reproduction of insects, many of which are harmful to humans. The wet season characteristic of Florida's long summer would have also had negative health implications. Mosquitoes and flies are more abundant during the wet season and many intestinal parasites are transmitted by means of contaminated water or soil. During the wet season, exposure to these vectors would increase.

The wet season would also have meant more time huddled inside against the weather, which would have aided the spread of respiratory infections. Respiratory transmission of disease occurs when infectious droplets are spread through coughing, sneezing, or direct contact. Colds, flu, and pneumonia, as well as many of the common childhood diseases, such as measles and mumps are spread by this means. The high temperature, humidity, and rainfall characteristic of Florida would have enabled many disease vectors to reproduce during much of the year, leaving the inhabitants of Windover susceptible to a number of infectious organisms.

Inadequate means of human waste disposal would also have played a role in the transmission of infectious organisms at Windover. Although no habitation sites were discovered indicating where the people of Windover were living in relation to the pond, we can be sure that the disposal of human waste was a constant challenge. If they were living close to the pond, the surrounding area would have served as a place for the disposal of waste. Human fecal matter, discarded food remains, and rotting fruit and meat would have provided ample means for the transmission of infectious organisms. The tropical pattern of rainfall seen in Florida, with its frequent heavy cloudbursts, can cause water runoff. If that water is contaminated, it can serve as a means of transmission for infectious organisms. Soil contamination from waste would have put individuals in close contact with pathogens. The environments associated with hunter-gatherer people would have posed considerable challenges to those dependent on the natural world around them.

Seasonal use of sites can also result in seasonal shortages of food, should environmental factors such as drought or flooding affect availability. These fluctuations, which can affect both quantity and quality of food, can have negative effects on growth and health, especially among children.

Biological stress can prolong infectious processes and increase recovery time. The diet of hunter-gatherers is precarious and highly dependent upon environmental and seasonal stability. Shifts in resource availability could impact the entire population, one individual at a time. Resource variability would require social response to solve issues of shortage.

The excellent preservation afforded at Windover has provided a rare glimpse of life and health in ancient Florida. By comparing what we find at Windover to indicators of illness and injury among other populations, both contemporaneous and from other time periods, we can better understand changes in health that have taken place throughout human history. But how did the people of Windover handle the health challenges of seven thousand years ago? Our final chapter will explore this issue.

Evidence for Medicine

Plants are the most ancient form of medicine known. Archaeological evidence for the medicinal exploitation of plants goes back over five thousand years. Windover predates these accounts by two millennia. Over thirty different types of plants were identified at Windover, some from the abdominal areas of individuals. For some, these seed caches form the tangible remains of their last meal. For others, perhaps their last attempt at quelling the disease processes that led to their death. Black gum, wax myrtle and arrowhead were just some of the nineteen medicinal plants identified during excavation at Windover. By examining the types of pathologies experienced by the Windover population and the types of plants recovered, we can infer medicinal plant usage on a broad scale. By examining seed caches and pathologies of individual burials, we glimpse an intimate struggle for survival.

Burial 125, a woman in her sixties, suffered from severe arthritis of the spine and possible bone cancer. She was found with a large concentration of elderberry seeds in her belly, along with grape seeds, nightshade, and prickly pear. Elderberry has edible seeds that are known for their analgesic and antirheumatic properties, as is nightshade. Perhaps she consumed these plants as an attempt at end-of-life pain relief.

One hundred twenty seven grape seeds were recovered from the belly region of Burial 93, a woman in her fifties. Examination of her skeleton reveals a possible cancerous lesion on her skull, along with a compression fracture of her spine and a healed fracture of her arm. Grape seed is used in a number of therapeutic ways. It is a natural pain reliever and used to treat diarrhea and other gastrointestinal problems. The large concentration of grape seeds indicates she either ate a large amount just prior to death, which is unlikely, or ingested them for their medicinal properties.

The pain relief properties of grape may have also been used for Burial 119, a man in his sixties suffering from extensive fusion of his spine from arthritis. The fused vertebrae rendered his spine immobile and he was unable to bend or flex side-to-side. He had also sustained two broken fingers during life, which may have added to his disabilities. One hundred ninety grape seeds were found in close association with his body.

Plants were not the only means of treating the ill or injured at Windover. Both archaeological and paleopathological evidence indicates they were splinting their broken bones. Fractures were a way of life among the Windover population and are found throughout their bodies. But most of their broken bones were not only well healed, they had healed in proper alignment. Pain at the site of the injury would have compelled the injured to immobilize the area. Immobilization would have reduced pain, minimized tissue damage surrounding the injury, and allowed the injury to heal in its proper position. The overwhelming number of fractures showing proper alignment indicates the people of Windover must have had knowledge of the therapeutic benefits of splinting and were using them to aid in the healing of their fractures.

The archaeological evidence for wood working is found in the graves themselves. Recall the wooden sticks that were erected over the bodies when they were placed in the pond, anchoring them to the base of the pond and protecting them from predators. This same woodworking ability would have been applied to the production of splints that were secured to an injured arm or leg. They may also have been creating slings out of the same woven fabrics used as burial shrouds. Slings would have enabled broken arms, shoulder blades, and collar bones, evidence for which are found among the Windover people, to heal in their proper position. This would have minimized healing time and reduced the chance of permanent disability.

Their material culture also holds clues to medicine, possibly in the form of ritual. Four intricately incised bone tubes, approximately five centimeters in length and made from bird bone, were recovered from burials within the pond. Bird bone tubes have been created and used by aboriginal people in many parts of the world, some of the oldest dating back to 9,000 BC, from Shanidar, Iraq. Ethnographic accounts describe how these tubes are commonly used in healing and ritual ceremonies, either to inhale smoke from fires to blow snuff or hallucinogens into the nose or in symbolic acts where a shaman or healer places the tube against a sick individual's skin to "suck" the infirmity from the victim.

At Windover, these tubes were recovered from the burials of three women and a child. Likewise, four turtle-shell containers, too small to be used for food preparation but possibly used for the preparation of medicines, were also recovered from the burials of three women and a child. On the South Pacific islands of Samoa, specialists known as *taulasea* are women trained in the location, identification, and administration of medicinal plants that grow wild on the islands. The training and skills are passed through the maternal line, with healers apprenticing under female family members or other specialists. The *taulasea* possess extensive knowledge about disease processes and the appropriate treatments for various pathologies. Perhaps at Windover, women practiced similar traditions and were tasked with gathering, preparing, and administering medicines to the sick.

The tube and container recovered from the children's graves may have been used in an attempt to cure them. The child buried with the turtle shell container suffered from nutritional deficiency during his two years of life. The four-year-old child buried with the bird bone tube had broken his clavicle. Their causes of death remain a mystery.

The skeletons themselves hold the most striking evidence for medicine. Many exhibit long-term illness or injury that would have required not only assistance from other members of the group, but also some form of treatment to enable them to survive for so long. Burial 72, a middle-aged woman who sustained a fractured femur earlier in life, would have been unable to walk for many weeks while the bone slowly mended. Burial 119, the elderly man whose immobile spine kept him in a permanent stooped position, could not have survived without the help of others. The many children showing signs of malnutrition would have needed extra attention to enable them to make it through their difficult early years when they were most susceptible to death. Many didn't make it, but the ones who did reveal the hardy nature of a people surviving in a hostile environment.

One of the most dramatic examples of long-term care is a young boy with spina bifida. His disabilities were extensive, his body emaciated and ravaged by infection. Yet he survived for almost 18 years. Someone took care of him, bringing him food and water, cleaning him and providing clothing and shelter. They carried him when the group moved and may have even assisted in the amputation his foot. The bones of his right lower leg are cloaked with the reactive bone of systemic infection. His skeleton has no right ankle; the leg bones taper to withered, deformed points. His foot, deprived of adequate blood flow due to the massive infection in his leg, may have slowly rotted away. Perhaps someone within the group removed the dead tissue, wrapping what was left. Pre-Columbian evidence for amputation spans North, Central, and South America and is found among artistic renderings and on skeletons in the form of disarticulated joints and missing extremities, testaments to this early form of treatment.

Even the burials at Windover attest to the care and concern they shared for each other. Great care was taken in the treatment of the dead. No clues remain as to body preparation, such as treating the body with herbs or mineral pigments, but great care was taken in placing the bodies in the pond.

Bodies were carried into the shallow margins of the pond, beyond the thick tangles of tree roots. Once the body was pushed into the soft soils of the pond, a small tipi-like construction of branches was erected over the body. The wood used for these shelters was primarily ash. Ash does not naturally occur near the pond and appears to have been chosen specifically for this purpose. Perhaps this type of wood held ceremonial significance. Singular wooden stakes possibly marked the location of individual graves or family units.

The pond itself may have held ritual significance for the people of Windover. Radiocarbon dating shows they returned to the pond for up to one thousand years. Its continued use may have been due to its close proximity to favorable hunting territory. Perhaps they returned to the area because of the significance of the pond. We will never know why they chose this pond. All we can affirm is its recurring ceremonial use as a sacred site for the interment of the dead.

The people from Windover could have chosen to dispose of their dead by placing them in the woods, far from their living sites. They could have burned the remains to avoid the unpleasantness of decomposition. Or they could have merely abandoned the dead and moved on. Instead, they took great pains in wrapping the dead, placing intricate tools and decorative items that were used or treasured in life alongside the bodies and carefully submerging them beneath the surface of the pond. The care they exhibited in death was possibly an extension of the care they showed each other in life. Their resourcefulness in exploiting the natural world around them for the care and treatment of the sick serves as one of the most ancient examples of medicine in human history.

CONCLUSION

Today, when I stand on the shores of Windover Pond, I think about the people from Windover. I look out over its surface and wonder at the life histories that ended along the edges of this small body of water. The limbs of encroaching oaks reach down to graze the pale green mat of algae that covers its surface. The muddy shores taper into the shallows and Spanish moss drapes the stark limbs, casting flowing shadows over the pond's surface. The air is cold and the sounds of civilization are muffled by the surrounding woods. I stand where many stood thousands of years ago. This pond held the remains of their people—their parents, their siblings, their children. Its meaning remains a mystery steeped in the shallow waters. But meaning it must have had, for the people of Windover returned to this pond for many generations, laying the bodies of their dead beneath its murky surface.

The pond is now a protected archaeological site. It represents a people far removed from Florida's history. But something of them lingers in the woods around the pond. Their voices were once carried by the winds from the Atlantic. Their fears once lurked in the shadows beyond their firelight. Their thoughts followed their loved ones to the grave, as each body was carefully placed beneath the surface. And there, tucked within the dark waters, their history lives on.

INDEX

R

R.L. Andrews Center for Perishables Analysis, 101
radiocarbon, 26, 84
radiocarbon dating, 26
radius, 26
rank, 23
reconstructing, 59, 61, 65
reconstruction, 59, 88, 118
red mulberry, 85
red-brown peat, 84
Republic Groves, 52
respiratory infections, 130
restoration, 59
rib, 26
ritual, 22, 46, 106
riverine, 118
robust, 6, 61, 62, 109
robusticity, 61
Roplex, 57, 58, 59
Royal, Bill, 51
rubber peat, 84

S

sacred, 23
sand, 34, 35, 37, 59, 84, 93, 126
sandals, 101
saw palmetto, 85, 104
school visits, 77
scrapers, 94
screens, 40, 67, 74
sea level, 129
seasonal, 86, 118, 131
seasonal fluctuations, 86, 118
seasonality, 85
sedentary, 111
seeds, 29, 84, 85, 96
sequences, 45, 64
sex, 6, 61, 62, 107, 108, 109, 110, 111
sexing, 61, 62
shaft straighteners, 94
shark's tooth, 96
shell, 88, 96, 104
shells, 96
shorelines, 83
shovel shaves, 38
shovel test, 36

shovel testing, 35, 37
sieves, 84
Sigler-Eisenberg, Brenda, 21, 22, 23
Silver Springs, 90
skeletal biology, 64
skeletal material, 25, 31, 66
skin color, 110
skull, 3, 4, 8, 19, 24, 42, 44, 45, 47, 51, 59, 61, 108, 109, 110, 116, 119
society, 22, 23
solution, 54, 56, 103
spear, 72, 92
spina bifida, 6, 135
spiritual, 23
splinting, 133
spoil, 8, 19, 25, 52, 63
spoil pile, 8
spun, 104
St. Johns River, 10
stabilization, 56, 103
stabilizing, 57, 59
stable isotope, 58, 118
Staphylococcus, 114
statistical, 110
status, 22
Stone Age, 73
stone points, 24, 37, 90, 93
Stone, Tammy, 74
Streptococcus, 114
stress, 115, 119, 121, 125, 131
string, 39, 96
submerged, 105
subsistence, 125
subtropical, 129
sulfur, 47
surface water, 83
suture closures, 108
Swann, Jim, 7, 9, 10, 11, 12, 13, 14, 19, 20, 21, 23, 26, 27, 30, 32, 35, 54, 55, 64
switch cane, 85
syphilis, 115
systemic infection, 115

T

taeniasis, 129
Tallahassee, 7, 26, 57, 70
Tanner, Bill, 7, 13, 15, 17, 32